WATERF

with Tomás McCarthy

www.**HERO**BOOKS.digital

HEROBOOKS

PUBLISHED BY HERO BOOKS
1 WOODVILLE GREEN
LUCAN
CO. DUBLIN
IRELAND

Hero Books is an imprint of Umbrella Publishing
First Published 2021
Copyright © Tomás McCarthy 2021
All rights reserved

A CIP record for this book is available from the British Library

ISBN 9781910827406

Cover design and formatting: jessica@viitaladesign.com
Ebook formatting: www.ebooklaunch.com
Photographs: Sportsfile and Nigel Kelly

★ DEDICATION ★

To Mam and Dad, and my sisters Áine, Róisín and Ailís.
To Waterford supporters all over the world.

★ CONTENTS ★

★ ACKNOWLEDGEMENTS ★

THE WATERFORD PLAYERS are the stars of this book.

I was blown away by the response I got from every one of them. Thirty of them generously gave me their time over the past year and all spoke with such honesty about their careers. I was the lucky one to be at the end of the phone, and to be recording their stories. I learned something new from every conversation. Thank you all for sharing your memories.

Thanks to Liam Hayes and Hero Books for putting their faith in me for a second time. The *Game Of My Life* series is a wonderful way to remember the great GAA days for each county and I was delighted to get the call.

Thanks to all the people who helped me track down these Waterford greats. Phil Fanning in the *News & Star*, WLR commentator Kieran O'Connor, and county treasurer John Jackson were always at the end of the phone. These three men have given me so much assistance over the years.

Thanks also to Jonathan Downey in Erins Own, Paudie Coffey in Portlaw, and Michael Murphy in Passage for steering me in the right direction. A special mention to Mick Durand for helping me organise an interview with Tom Cunningham. Two gentlemen.

Thanks to Ger Lawton in the *News & Star*, a top man and a top sports editor who gave me a 'break' in 2010. I will never forget that.

To Nigel Kelly, Gavin Whelan, Julie Smyth and Michael Byrne in WLR for all your support and giving me the opportunity to cover matches and present a weekly GAA show. Nigel's photos of the 1959 heroes were much appreciated.

My parents have been behind me every step of the way.

My dad, Pat brought me to my first GAA match in 1998. What a summer to start supporting Waterford! I was hooked after that. We followed the team all over the country… championship games, league games, South East league games, pitch openings… you name it.

My mam, Margaret gave me my interest in reading and writing, and for that I will be forever grateful. The radio is always on in our house and there's always newspapers around the place!

I love you both.

To my sisters Áine, Róisín and Ailís for your constant support. I'm so proud of you.

To my amazing girlfriend Brenda for backing me in everything I do and keeping me going during the Covid lockdowns.

To Waterford supporters… I hope you enjoy this book and the *great* memories from Waterford's *greats*!

Tomás McCarthy
September 2021

TOM CUNNINGHAM
(& MICHAEL O'CONNOR)

WATERFORD 1-11 CORK 1-6
Munster SHC Final
Thurles Sportsfield
JULY 14, 1957

A free-flowing Munster final against Cork in 1957, two years before the glory of '59, is the game that Tom Cunningham (above, centre) remembers most fondly from his illustrious career.

★ **WATERFORD:** D Roche; **T Cunningham**, A Flynn, J Barron; **M O'Connor**, M Morrissey, M Lacey; P Grimes (0-6), J O'Connor; M Flannelly (1-2), T Cheasty, F Walsh; S Power (0-1), J Kiely, L Guinan (0-1). Sub: D Whelan (0-1) for J O'Connor.

★ **CORK:** M Cashman; J Brohan, J Lyons, A O'Shaughnessy; P Dowling, V Twomey, M Fouhy; D O'Driscoll, E Goulding (0-1); M O'Regan (1-1), WJ Daly (0-1), C O'Shea (0-1); F O'Mahony, T Kelly (0-1), P Barry. Subs: P Healy (0-1) for O'Mahony, N Looney for Twomey.

THE ACTION

A THIRD MUNSTER title for Waterford and a first since 1948 in front of an attendance of 39,254. Only the brilliance of Cork goalkeeper Mick Cashman prevented a heavier defeat for the Rebels.

Pat Fanning from Mount Sion took over as chairman of the Waterford County Board in 1957. In a famous speech at Fraher Field, he gathered the players together and told them that there was an All-Ireland in the team. The Déise defeated Limerick in the first round of the Munster Championship (4-12 to 5-5) as Dick Roche, Joe Harney, Mick Lacey and Larry Guinan all made their debuts.

Cork legend Christy Ring sat out the final after he broke his wrist in their semi-final win over Tipperary. He watched on from the sidelines, as the Rebels played with a strong wind in the first-half but shot 11 wides and trailed by a point at the break.

It took 20 minutes for the first point to arrive through Déise forward Larry Guinan, when he had the goal at his mercy. Philly Grimes added a gem of a point. Terry Kelly opened Cork's account on 22 minutes before Eamon Goulding equalised.

Seamus Power palmed the ball over the bar to leave Waterford 0-3 to 0-2 ahead at halfway. On the resumption, Cork edged ahead for the first time through a free from Christy O'Shea. Whelan levelled the game again. Ten minutes into the second-half, Mick Flannelly goaled for Waterford. Points from Grimes and Flannelly put Waterford out of reach. All-action midfielder Grimes was Man of the Match with six points (five points from placed balls).

Déise shot-stopper Dick Roche and corner-back Tom Cunningham scrambled away late Cork efforts at goal. Cunningham shadowed Rebel danger man Paddy Barry while wing back Michael O'Connor saw off both Christy O'Shea and Willie John Daly. Waterford went on to reach the All-Ireland final that September where they lost to Kilkenny by a point.

★ ★ ★ ★ ★

66

I STARTED MY senior hurling inter-county career in 1952 and it wasn't very organised until Pat Fanning and John Keane took over.

They introduced a system of collective training. In other words, we came together twice a week. Whereas before, it was more or less off-the-cuff, fellas nearly trained on their own. I don't remember training before that as a group. We generally trained down in Walsh Park; they gave us tea and sandwiches after in the dressing-rooms.

Fanning was the man that did the talking, and John Keane was more laid-back. The first time we gathered for training over in Fraher Field, Pat gathered us around in the middle of the field in a circle. He was impressing upon us that we were as good as any other team in Ireland and there was no reason why we couldn't win an All-Ireland. That was 1957.

Before that, we were regarded as underdogs against most teams, particularly all the teams in Munster. Pat was impressing upon us how good we were. He was praising us. We had no reason to feel like second-class citizens compared to the other teams in Munster or Leinster. We were as good if not better than most of the other teams and there was no reason why we couldn't win an All-Ireland. We shouldn't have any doubts about our own abilities.

That was his mantra.

When you win the All-Ireland, that's obviously one of your favourites but the match I remember most is my first Munster final in 1957 against Cork.

Waterford and Cork were playing this free-flowing hurling as it became known after. It was a close match; we won by five points. At that time, there was no such thing as putting your hand up and catching the ball. That wasn't a feature of any team.

Wexford were the first team that handled a lot of the ball because they were all big men. In general, the ball didn't go as far then as it does now. All the balls now are passing over midfield, whereas back in the 50s it was a different type of ball so it was generally contested between the centrefielders. They contested it by pulling, for or against.

Ground hurling was the only hurling that was really known at the time, or...

moving the ball along. There was no such thing as handling the ball or passing it across; that didn't happen at all. It was all off-the-cuff stuff, if you like.

I was corner-back in 1957. I'd say my most dangerous opponent was Paddy Barry from Cork. He was a very skilful hurler; he wasn't interested in any physical stuff. He was the opposite to Christy Ring, who was skilful but more competitive! I'll put it that way! I didn't come up against Ring that often. I might have played on him once in 1962.

The general consensus was that I was a better footballer than a hurler! I wasn't too bad at *that* game either. Fellas would come along and say, 'You were always a better footballer than a hurler'. Whether I was or not, I don't know.

I didn't play any full match in the All-Ireland series or the Munster Championship in 1959. I had my wrist in plaster for two months. I played a part in the Munster final and the drawn All-Ireland final and I started the replay, but I suffered a half-accidental injury that forced me to retire!

Jim 'The Link' Walsh was full-back for Kilkenny. I think he hit me in the back of the head with the hurley! Something like that anyway! It wasn't a clash anyway; it was an off the ball thing. I got injured, I went to the Mater Hospital. I got my stitches in and I was sent back again. Getting stitched then was a common thing!

It wasn't unusual for fellas to end up with stitches. I missed the final whistle and the presentation of the cup. I have no recollection of it at all.

We did a tour with the cup in 1959.

We went to Dunhill, Kilmacthomas, Cappoquin, Lismore, Ballyduff... all the main clubs at the time and particularly the clubs that had a player on the team.

We played Cork in the Munster hurling final in 1959 and the following Sunday, I refereed the Munster football final between Kerry and Cork with my teammates Frankie Walsh and Larry Guinan as linesmen! I don't know did they ever do linesman before!

I refereed an All-Ireland football semi-final in 1960 between Down and Offaly. My refereeing didn't come in for a lot of compliments after it anyway! It was unusual at the time to give a penalty and I gave a penalty to Down. It was contentious.

The newspapers felt that it wasn't a penalty at all, that it should have been a free out. The match ended in a draw and Down went on to win the replay, and went on to win their first All-Ireland… which was the first All-Ireland for a Six County team. So, I had some bit of notoriety attached to it!

Philly Grimes was the greatest Waterford hurler I played with. He was a very skilful hurler and he was an athlete as well in terms of his build and his speed. He was well built; I'd say he was on the six foot mark. He was skilful and he was tough so he would have been my favourite.

In my own club, Dungarvan, John Kiely used to play full-forward. He would have been remembered for his toughness. He was small and he was grey-haired so he stood out. I would always go for Grimes. He had no notions about himself. He was very down to earth.

MICHAEL O'CONNOR

After defeating Cork in the 1957 Munster final, Michael O'Connor was hospitalised for six months with TB and feared his hurling career was at a premature end.

"

WE KNEW WE were a big force in the championship. The team was playing at such a high level of ground hurling.

I don't think Christy Ring was playing, but it was such a big achievement for Waterford to win a Munster Championship. I was wing back, playing No 5. I played alongside Martin Óg Morrissey and Philly Grimes in the half-back line. Outstanding players, both of them.

Philly Grimes was the greatest Waterford hurler I played with. He was an exceptional athlete as well as being a very good hurler.

When I was playing right half-back, Mickey Kelly of Kilkenny was my toughest opponent. He was a low gravity man about five foot eight or nine, very strong and when he got on the ball you couldn't take it off him.

We should have won in 1957. We had Kilkenny well beaten in the All-Ireland final; we were a couple of goals ahead with 10 or 15 minutes to go. We were completely in control of that game and we threw it away.

When I played that game, my family knew I had a problem because my brother-in-law was a doctor. My father still wanted me to play the All-Ireland final. I played that game and I shouldn't have been playing.

My father was a Cork man but he loved me playing for Waterford. He wanted me to play but he didn't want to tell me there was anything wrong. They waited until afterwards to tell me. Three weeks.

I was in hospital for six months with TB.

I felt that I'd be lucky to get out of it again.

I dreaded Covid-19. I knew what it was like to be locked up. It was a long time ago but it stays with me. A lot of people died around that time from TB. My mother died of TB. She was a young woman; I was only nine when she died.

These things were on my mind.

I was told by the doctors that my hurling days were over. I was told to be very careful and not to overdo things. I didn't get out until March 1958. Hurling was secondary at that stage.

At the end of '58, I started to play an odd match.

I was back on the Waterford panel in 1959, but I didn't play during the campaign. I only came on as a sub in the All-Ireland final. As an act of appreciation, I was picked as a selector so that kept me involved. I really looked up to the chairman Pat Fanning and the trainer John Keane. I had a good relationship with Pat.

I was reluctant to go on in the final but I was delighted to get the opportunity. I felt great but I had put on a bit of weight. My confidence wasn't as good.

I was marking Eddie Keher.

I remember going for the first ball on the wing. I rose the ball and gave a little swerve, and I thought that I would drive it into the opposition square but he was able to hook me. I was surprised at it. It was unbelievable.

That team continued on for four or five years. I retired after the 1959 All-Ireland final. I was 29 at that stage. I married Mary in 1960 and I didn't play anymore.

My father used to tell Mary, 'Would you stop baking, he has to train!' He still wanted me to play, but I felt that I wasn't up to it.

It was totally different in those days.

I went to a match up in the North of Ireland, up on a bus; it took us all day to get there; it was sleet and snow when we got there, there was nobody on the pitch only ourselves.

We were playing Antrim. I never hit the ball.

I couldn't even raise the hurley I was so cold! I was shaking! We were so dirty but we came up and home on the bus. No facilities.

The two passions in my life were hurling and hunting.

When I was younger, I used to go riding point-to-points. I got a pony. I loved it; I loved horses and ponies. The hurling took over then… I did one thing at a time!

Cappoquin had six players on the 1948 All-Ireland minor-winning team and the team trainer. *The Magnificent Seven.*

A local man, Jim Ahearne was his name; he took us to the field after school, three days a week and organised local matches when we were 14 or 15. His sister used to call me The Cappoquin Greyhound! I was very fast!

Mick Flannelly was one of my best friends on the Waterford team. Every team picture from 1947 on, I was next to Mick Flan. We played minor and senior; we played together for 10 years. We got on really well.

We always seemed to be next to each other in a photograph! Always.

We had a great understanding. When Flan got the ball, I knew where it was going to be hit. I couldn't hit the ball straight over the bar but he presented it so well to me, that I couldn't miss!

All of my medals were stolen 15 years ago.

We were cleaned out one night. We went into town and people broke into the place and stole everything we had. We got onto the GAA at the time and they replaced them.

I was proud to be a member of that team.

99

LARRY GUINAN

WATERFORD 9-3 TIPPERARY 3-4
Munster SHC Semi-Final
Cork Athletic Grounds
JULY 12, 1959

Three goals in the epic nine-goal victory over Tipperary in 1959 were savoured by Larry Guinan (on the left in the back row before the '59 Munster final), who always felt Tipp could never accept losing to Waterford.

★ **WATERFORD:** N Power; J Harney, A Flynn, J Barron; M Lacey, M Morrissey, J Condon; P Grimes, S Power (1-1); **L Guinan (3-0)**, T Cheasty, F Walsh (1-2); C Ware (2-0), D Whelan (1-0), J. Kiely (1-0). Subs: M Flannelly for Morrissey, M Morrissey for Power, S Power for Ware.

★ **TIPPERARY:** T Moloney; M Byrne, M Maher, K Carey; M Burns, T Wall (1-0), John Doyle; T English, D Nealon (1-2); Jimmy Doyle (1-2), L Devaney, G MacCarthy; M Maher, J McDonnell, W Moloughney. Subs: R Mounsey for Moloney, P Stakelum for McDonnell.

THE ACTION

A DAY OF days for Waterford hurling.

A never to be forgotten performance by the banks of the Lee as reigning league, Munster and All-Ireland champions Tipperary were beaten out the gate.

It was 8-2 to 0-0 at half-time. RTÉ commentator Michael O'Hehir didn't believe the scoreline when it was handed to him during his broadcast of the Leinster final at Croke Park. He sought clarification. A call was made to the garda barracks in Cork.

The previous summer, the Premier County defeated the Déise by 16 points in the Munster final (4-12 to 1-5). 'It was payback time,' said Seamus Power. 'They gave us a trouncing and we were determined to do the same to them.'

It was a traumatic result for Tipperary. 'I went home after that beating and spent the whole night crying,' admitted legendary forward Jimmy Doyle in later years.

Tipp won the toss and captain Tony Wall chose to play against a gale force wind in the first-half. They were hit by a Waterford whirlwind as Frankie Walsh, Larry Guinan, Donal Whelan, Charlie Ware, John Kiely and Seamus Power all found the net.

The Déise got seven goals against Galway in the first round of the Munster Championship but they had eight on the scoreboard by the 22nd minute. Martin Óg Morrissey came off with a head injury during that opening half and was replaced by Mick Flannelly. Seamus Power made way at the break with a leg injury and Morrissey returned to the field with his head bandaged. Tipp changed their goalkeeper, and centre-back Tony Wall moved into the attack.

It proved mission impossible for the Premier men. Donie Nealon, Jimmy Doyle and Tony Wall got consolation goals in the second period as they outscored their opponents 3-4 to 1-1. Mick Flannelly flicked the ball over John Doyle's head to Larry Guinan and the Mount Sion ace completed his hat-trick. Frankie Walsh pointed a late free to finish it off.

★★★★★

66

THE GAME AGAINST Tipperary below in Cork, that was my favourite game playing for Waterford. I was very pleased. That was a great win; it was great to beat Tipperary.

I scored three goals against John Doyle, a big, brute of a fella playing for Tipperary. He couldn't hurl all that well, but he was known as a famous player. I got three goals off him that day. I was very pleased about it, very happy.

The rivalry was fierce.

Tipp were bad losers. I always felt that they could never take it when they were beaten. I can remember Tony Wall saying to me, after beating them twice… coming off the field saying, 'We'll meet ye again… we'll meet ye again'. That was their attitude.

We'll meet ye again to beat ye kind of thing.

They didn't beat us. We beat them the third time, which was the Oireachtas final in Croke Park. That's the way it was. I was very pleased when we beat Tipp.

Cork were a lovely crowd. I always found Cork a good crowd and could take their beating and shake hands.

There was a fierce wind in Cork that day.

8-2 to 0-0 at half-time. Michael O Hehir came on the radio. 'I have a score below in Cork between Waterford and Tipperary. Waterford 8-2, Tipperary 0-0… Oh God, I don't know if that's right, I'll have to check that and come back with that score.'

He came back on the radio and said, 'Yes, it's true!'

Tony Wall was a great centre-back for Tipperary for years. Believe it or not, he rang me just recently and he said, 'You know the thing I can always remember about hurling is the beating ye gave us. I'll never forgive ye for that… the beating ye gave us below in Cork.'

I hadn't seen or spoken to Tony in 50 years, I suppose. He was an army man. He rang me to congratulate us on getting to an All-Ireland final.

We were rampant. We were going well and we thought we would never get enough of the ball. We felt so, so confident. We wanted to rattle them and we did.

We felt good about it and we thought the longer it would go on, the more we'd beat them by… 8-2 to 0-0… I'll never forget it.

I was very happy with that.

I remember Frank Walsh and myself; Frankie was captain. He was a great captain. I remember Frankie and myself up in Walsh Park and we were training and we were crossing the ball from one side to the other, and we had this thing off to perfection.

Frankie got the ball out on the left wing and crossed it right over and put it to perfection to me, and I stretched out and tapped the ball into the goal. I remember that distinctly. I remember looking over at Frank and putting up the hurl.

That was a great memory from 1959.

The balls were like big, wet sods. It was mostly ground hurling. John Keane was our trainer. He had us above in Walsh Park and he said, 'All I want to see is ground hurling, no one to pick a ball'.

This ball came across to me and it bounced; sometimes it would hit the sod and jump into your hand. I put out the hand and by God did I get it from Keane that day! *Oh Jesus! He read me the riot act! I'll never forget it.*

That's what we were doing, it was mostly ground hurling at that time. It was different than today. At that time, if you put your hand up to catch a ball, all hell could break loose. You would be pulling on a ball and if a fella put up his hand, well then, he had to suffer the consequences.

That's the way it was. There wasn't much catching at that time; it was pulling in the air really… a high ball coming in and two fellas clashing. Now, it's all fellas putting up their hands and grabbing balls.

I got a fair few belts and a fair few stitches, but I didn't mind that. Believe it or not, I never got a broken bone. I don't know why but I never got a broken bone.

Jimmy Doyle of Tipperary was the best I played on.

Jimmy was a lovely hurler. He got a fair few goals off me at one stage in Ferrybank; we were playing them in a tournament. He was very good. I remember my first time playing for Waterford, at minor, we played Tipperary above in Limerick. Jimmy gave an exhibition the same day. He was by far the best.

I never played on Ring so I wouldn't know, but Jimmy Doyle was the best I played on.

Frankie was the best I played with. The thing about Frankie and myself… Seamus Power and Philly Grimes were there for years and years and they couldn't win anything. They couldn't win anything until we came along, the two young fellas… Frankie and myself!

We always said that to them after!

They couldn't win anything until we came along and that's the size of it! Frankie to me was the best. He was a great captain and a great hurler.

After we won the All-Ireland, myself and Frankie had a photo taken below in Annie Brophy's, a famous photographer at the time. She was known all over the country. Seamus and Philly got a photo taken with their Munster jerseys, so Frankie and myself had to go and we decided that we'd wear the Waterford jerseys!

We went out to Annie Brophy's and she had put in new lino on the floor. Frankie and myself togged out to get the photo taken and, by Jaysus, all I could feel was the bloody lino… and I digging into it with the cogs and the boots! I remember that well! She looked at it and she said, 'Oh Jesus, my God almighty! What will I do? I'm only after putting this down'.'

That's where we got the photo taken, it was a lovely photo. We went out with our Waterford jerseys, so again we had one up on them which was great!

I got my debut in 1957. Waterford were playing Kilkenny in Walsh Park in a league game. I wasn't even on the panel or anything. I was only a young fella and I never thought I'd make a Waterford senior hurler.

Pat Fanning knocked on my door one morning, around 11 or 12 o'clock, and he said 'Larry, would you play for Waterford today?'

I said, 'I will… I will!' I was delighted!

I was only a little bit of a fella and when we went out, we were playing Kilkenny and it was a wicked bad day, Jaysus…' twas an awful day!

I was playing on a fella called Link Walsh. He must have been about 18 stone! On a little fella like me on a muddy day! I remember this ball coming down, a high ball, and I pulled on it and I must have knocked out a few of his teeth!

He caught my hurley and threw it into the crowd and beat me with the hurley. I had a sore backside that day alright! I remember that well. That was my debut. We got an awful beating, a wicked beating. That was February and by the end of that year, I was playing in an All-Ireland final.

We played Galway in the semi-final. That was my first time seeing Croke Park. We were in the dressing-room and I remember coming out onto the field… *Jesus, I shook out… I shook out.* There was a fella by the name of Fives. He pulled a dirty stroke on Frank even though he was an ex-Waterford man.

I went over; I always backed up Frankie. Frankie was a lovely fella and he wouldn't retaliate as such. I had a bit of a temper and I went over and I gave your man a wicked belt alright across the arse! I did!

The game was only on and I had the ball in the goal. I scored the first goal of the match that day.

My father worked on the Great Western ship.

No one had anything at that time. They were tough times. I had been in and out of a few little jobs. I was a messenger boy; at times I used to be delivering chickens to people in Tramore and up in John's Hill… they were the only people that could afford it.

I used to be the messenger boy for Flanagans and Powers. I used to go on the train, the Tramore train… I used to go on that with my bike and deliver the chickens. I went down this day and I got my ticket to go on the Great Western that night. I was going away to England. I was coming up the quay… and I met Pat Fanning and Mick Miniter.

Mick Miniter was a detective in town at the time. A lovely man.

We stopped to have a chat for a minute. I said to Pat that I was going away tonight. Pat freaked out.

'Why? What's wrong?'

I told him, 'Look Pat, I'm only doing messenger boy work here. I want to do something for myself. The people at home could do with a few bob.'

The two of them started talking to each other and they told me to hold on for a few minutes. They went across the road and after a little while they said to me, 'Would you take a job if you got it Monday?'

'Would I?' I said.

'Well you can start Monday in A.B.E.' I went to A.B.E. and I started for Mr Nugent. I was there for 10 years and I enjoyed every bit of it. That's what made me stay… and then I got onto the Waterford team.

I decided to go into the tyres so I opened up here and I never looked back, thanks to be to God. I'm flying now at the moment.

I'm still up at six o'clock every morning. I open up the place, get it ready, get the machinery ready for the lads… clean up the mess made the day before and whatever.

That's what I still do.

99

MARTIN ÓG MORRISSEY

WATERFORD 4-12 TIPPERARY 3-9
Oireachtas Final
Croke Park
OCTOBER 21, 1962

Four times in the space of 12 months, Waterford defeated Tipperary, but the Oireachtas final win in 1962 was Martin Óg Morrissey's best display against the Premier County. Here Martin is photographed second from right in the front row before the 1959 Munster final.

★ **WATERFORD:** N Power; T Cunningham, A Flynn, J Byrne; L Guinan, **M Óg Morrissey**, J Irish; M Dempsey, J Condon (0-4); M Flannelly (0-1), T Cheasty (0-1), F Walsh (1-1); S Power, J Barron (2-2), P Grimes (1-3).

★ **TIPPERARY:** R Mounsey; M Hassett, M Maher, K Carey; M Burns, T Wall (0-1), C Hartigan; T English, D Nealon (2-1); J Doyle (0-4), J McKenna (1-3), T Ryan; L Devaney, T Moloughney, S McLoughlin. Sub: R McElgunn for Burns.

THE ACTION

'PORT LÁIRGE ABÚ,' roared Waterford captain Larry Guinan as he got his hands on the Oireachtas trophy in the Hogan Stand. Waterford exacted revenge on All-Ireland champions Tipperary for a humiliating Munster final loss earlier in the season before a crowd of 20,108. The Premier County prevailed by 20 points in the provincial decider in August (5-14 to 2-3). October 21 was a day of redemption for the Déise.

Martin Óg Morrissey had his finest hour in a Waterford shirt. The Mount Sion centre-back was indestructible. The mighty No 6 knocked over Tipp forwards like skittles. In one power play, he smashed Liam Devaney and John McKenna before he cleared the sliotar 70 metres down the field. He gave an exhibition of ground hurling that afternoon.

Waterford held a narrow 1-5 to 1-4 advantage at half-time. Two minutes in, Tipperary goalkeeper Roger Mounsey saw a low shot from Frankie Walsh fly between his legs. Tipp, who took the field without John Doyle, had 12 first-half wides compared to Waterford's two. Jimmy Doyle crossed and Donie Nealon goaled for the Premier just before the break.

The blue and gold edged a point up early in the second period. Déise midfielder Joe Condon responded with two points. The Erins Own man took charge of that sector. He knocked over four long range efforts in total.

Seamus Power and Philly Grimes combined to set up John Barron for Waterford's second goal. They added another off the next attack. Grimes collected a delivery from Condon on this occasion and beat Mounsey (3-8 to 1-6). John McKenna got a goal and a point for Tipp. Points by Condon, Grimes and Barron sent Waterford seven clear.

Donie Nealon lashed a 21-yard free to the roof of the net for the Premier men. His second goal of the afternoon. Barron buried his second major in the last minute after he ran onto a ball from Grimes. A first Oireachtas title for Waterford.

★★★★★

❝

IT WAS PROBABLY the best game I played with Waterford.

I'll tell you a little story about that match. We came in after the match, into the dressing-room, and we were putting on our clothes. I was facing the wall and taking whatever it was off the hanger and I got a tap on the shoulder.

Austin Flynn was there; put out his hand and shook hands with me.

'Thanks for medal,' he said.

He went back to Dungarvan anyway and he was telling people what happened. 'You know what Óg said to me,' he told them… "Where's the other thirteen?"'

I won 21 medals in the one day!

In 1963, in the space of 12 months, we beat Tipperary four times. It was never heard tell of before, or after I'd say. The Munster final was the last one we played them in. We were coming off the field and Tony Wall said to Philly Grimes, 'Ye we're lucky today!'

And Grimes turned around and said, 'That's the fourth time we're after beating ye this year!'

I was marking John 'Mackey' McKenna that day. I met him at the launch of Jimmy Doyle's book and I was talking to him. He turned around and pointed at me and he said, 'Do you see that fella there? That was the best centre-back I ever played on'.

I was a hurling centre half-back.

Jimmy Hegarty was a goalie with Galway around that time.

He was down in Waterford a couple of years ago and he came out to see me. I hadn't a clue who the chap was when he came in.

'The old Galway people talking about hurling said that you were the first hurling centre half-back they ever saw.'

I take it they must have been talking about mullakers before that!

We played fast, open hurling. We let the ball do the work. You didn't hang onto it, you got rid of it.

Paddy Barry of Cork was my toughest opponent. He was a big man but he was a good hurler too. He reckoned he was as good as Christy Ring. He was a good hurler and he was a big strong man into the bargain.

I enjoyed playing in Croke Park. As a matter of fact, I don't think I had a bad match in Croke Park. I played well in them all.

The 1959 All-Ireland final was a fair auld game. We should have won the first day. It was 18 scores to 10… 1-17 to 5-5. We scored more times than Kilkenny did but they were getting goals and we were getting points.

In the replay… after five minutes I knew we'd win it. The ball was running in our favour that day.

Pat Fanning was a good chairman of the County Board. Up to the time Pat became chairman, when you went away to play a match, you might get a cup of tea and a sandwich. When he took over as chairman, he brought us into a hotel and we were given a good feed.

He looked after us well alright.

We could have won another three or four All-Irelands.

With a little bit of luck, we would have won more. As Johnny McGovern said to me at Paddy Buggy's funeral, 'If you got two more balls in 1963, Waterford would have won the match'.

Philly Grimes was the greatest Waterford hurler I played with. He was an all-round athlete; he had speed, he had skill. He was a lovely hurler so he was.

I remember coming across the bridge on a lorry down the Quay and into the Town Hall for a Mayoral Reception. There was a councillor there at the time; the Bully Man was his nickname, James Power his real name. He was giving a bit of a speech during the reception.

He said, 'Not alone are they the best team in Ireland, they are the best team in Europe!'

We went from that then into the Olympia. Oh, it was packed. Packed out the door, so it was. There was some crowd there that night.

We went all around the county with the cup. We went everywhere. We were in Dunhill, Kilmacthomas, Dungarvan, Cappoquin… I can't remember all the places we were. They looked after us well after we won the All-Ireland.

John Keane was a good trainer.

He never roared at anybody. I never saw him losing his cool with us. If he thought you were doing something wrong, he would walk over and just say it to you. I remember coming out of Walsh Park one day... I was walking down Slievekeale and he said, 'Another game or two like that and you'll be up with the greats like myself!'

John Keane was one of the *greats*. He hurled the ears off Mick Mackey from Limerick, probably the only centre half-back that ever did that.

The nicest hurler that I ever saw playing was a fella called Jimmy Langton from Kilkenny. In Waterford, the man I looked up to played with Mount Sion, Waterford and Munster... a fella called Paddy Dowling. He could hit a ball no matter where it was; if it was on the tip of his toes.

He had only one fault. He used to wear a cap and if the cap fell off, he would go for the cap before he would go for the ball! He was a beautiful hurler. Class to perfection.

99

JIM GREENE
(& PAT MCGRATH)

WATERFORD 4-9 CORK 3-8
Munster SHC First Round
Walsh Park
MAY 19, 1974

Upsetting the odds against newly crowned league champs Cork in the 1974 Munster Championship is the one game that Jim Greene will never forget (above, being presented to the crowd during a 'Stars of the 80s' celebration in Croke Park during the 2013 All-Ireland final).

★ **WATERFORD:** P Flynn; M Kirwan, P Coady, S Hannon; P Kelly, **J Greene**, **P McGrath**; J Galvin (0-1), A Heffernan; T Reide (1-0), M Hickey, P O'Grady (0-6); M Ormonde (1-1), J Kirwan (0-1), M Geary (2-0). Subs: S Greene for Heffernan, L Canning for Reide.

★ **CORK:** Paddy Barry; T Maher, M O'Doherty, J Horgan; Pat Barry, B Murphy, C Roche (0-1); D Coughlan, P Hegarty; T O'Brien, C McCarthy (1-4), G McCarthy (1-1); S O'Leary (1-1), M Malone (0-1), E O'Donoghue. Subs: M Coleman for Pat Barry, J McCarthy for G McCarthy, J Buckley for Murphy.

THE ACTION

A MASSIVE UPSET. League champions Cork were knocked out of Munster in dramatic fashion before 13,000 spectators at Walsh Park as Rebel goalkeeper Paddy Barry was sent off two minutes before half-time.

Barry broke his hurley as Martin Geary forced home Waterford's third goal of the afternoon. He threw away the heavy end of his stick in disgust and it struck umpire Jim Kirby from Limerick in the thigh. Barry ran over and apologised but referee Sean O'Grady gave the Cork No 1 his marching orders. Defender Con Roche manned the goal for the remainder of the first-half.

The majestic Pat McGrath was given the role of extra man for Waterford, which he excelled in. McGrath was a big presence in the 70s and 80s for club, county and province and was unlucky to miss out on an All Star. He captained the Déise to the Munster under-21 title later that summer. Mount Sion clubmate Jim Greene also cut off the supply to the Cork forwards at centre-back. He finished his inter county career in the Waterford attack and won an All Star at corner-forward in 1982.

Two goals from Geary and one from Michael Ormonde left the Déise 3-4 to 1-3 in front at the break. Gerald McCarthy's shot from 35 yards out dropped into the Waterford net.

A Charlie McCarthy goal early in the second-half closed the gap to two points (3-4 to 2-5). Waterford responded with four points in-a-row including three frees from Pat O'Grady. A Seanie O'Leary goal left just a point between them. In the 48th minute, Pat McGrath supplied Tony Reide for the Déise's fourth and decisive goal.

Just like 1967, Waterford turned over a 14-man Cork outfit in Walsh Park. It was their biggest championship win of the 70s.

★ ★ ★ ★ ★

66

IN MY TIME, we didn't win anything really. We won half a league one time coming out of the second division, that was about the size of it. We had some great days in Munster; we got to Munster finals, got destroyed in the two of them but the semi-finals were memorable.

Cork were the dogs in those days, Cork were huge. They had a super team; they had about 20 All Stars… they had All Stars that were subs on the team! We were never really good enough. We never came out of Munster, sure. We never played Kilkenny in the championship. We never got to test ourselves any further than Munster.

That was as far as we went.

We beat Cork in 1974 in the Munster Championship which was huge. I was centre-back in those days. That was one of the best, that day we beat Cork in Walsh Park.

We had no chance. Seamus Power was our selector at the time. There was no such thing as managers and trainers. Seamus, who was on the 1959 team, he was our motivator and by Jesus he had us up for it that day.

It was a fabulous win against all the odds. Walsh Park was packed to the rafters. There was a brilliant atmosphere. It was all standing; there were no stands. It was all banks, so you fitted a lot more.

I was in the half-back line from 1968 up to about '76 and then I went to the forward line, and I got up to 1986 out of that. They're chalk and cheese. Underage, minor and under-21 for the county and senior with the club, I was centre-forward and centre-back. They couldn't make up their mind!

And I didn't mind as long as I was playing.

My first championship game was against Tipp in 1969 in Walsh Park. I was wing back; I marked Francis Loughnane and Jimmy Doyle for a half each! It was a daunting experience for an 18 or 19-year-old.

The Cork goalkeeper Paddy Barry was sent off. I think he was sent off in the wrong. The ball went into the net. My reckoning is he struck the umpire but I think he was striking the upright in temper; the umpire got in the way and he got sent off for it.

That was my reading of it at the time. Sure, Paddy Barry wasn't a dirty hurler. He was a very good goalkeeper. He wouldn't be like that. It was a great Cork team. We were way underdogs that day; that was some win for Waterford. Completely outside the norm.

We played Limerick in the next round in Thurles.

We had Limerick beaten that day… and they went on to play in the All-Ireland. They were a good side, Richie Bennis and all of those. They had a very good team and we had them beaten. We were about six or seven points up with eight or nine minutes to go and they got one lucky goal… and then a good goal which brought them right back into it and they pipped us in the end.

We had them on the rack; we should have taken it. We really should have but we didn't. That was the story of our lives at that stage.

In the early stages of my career, I was socialising and I was drinking up to 1976. I hit a crunch in 1976 and it was a defining moment. *I either take this serious or I don't.* So, I gave up drink completely. I was struggling at the game. I was drinking way too heavy.

When I came out of it, I went to AA.

That doesn't bother me people knowing that; it's not a problem at all. I spent a couple of years with them trying to clear myself and get myself right… and I *got* myself right. I ended up playing with Munster, I ended up getting an All Star, lots of things happened after that period.

I became very serious about my game. I lost a lot of weight, I got right serious about myself. The rest was history really.

The second half of my career was way more successful than the first half.

I was a new man. I was three stone lighter! I was gone wicked heavy, I needed to do something, like. When I came back, I more or less came back as a forward. With the club, half my career was in the half-back line and half my career was in the forward line.

At that stage, I was playing in the forwards for the club and I was doing alright; we were winning championships. We used to win fairly regularly in those days. Any accolades I got, I got them after that. It's obvious sure, it makes perfect sense.

You can't do two things. You can but you won't do any of them properly.

Nowadays, it's different. You'd be going to a gym.

My name is Jim… that's the closest I got to a gym!

Coaches were for travelling on! It was a different world completely. The game was different as well, much tougher, much harder, much more physical. Today, the game is much faster. It's played at a different pace and it's played in a different way as well.

We had fellas that had pace as well. I wouldn't have been a big pace man. I remember Eddie Nolan, Pat Curran… flyers now. There would be no one on the Waterford team today faster than those chaps. Pat McGrath was a flyer. An unbelievable half-back. One of the great tragedies of that time was that man not getting an All Star.

That was absolutely ridiculous. I could never understand that.

Pat McGrath was special. A big physical man and a flyer. He would outrun anybody Mac. And great skill, he could hit the ball eight or 10 different ways. Ken had the same ability. You'd never catch Ken. No matter what way he threw the ball, he struck it.

We were serious about our game. We did our three or four nights a week but after the match it would be common to celebrate, even if you were beaten. It was more acceptable in those days. It was an amateur sport played by amateurs and lived accordingly.

We gave it our best shot.

It's nearly professional now. Chaps have to watch the colour of their pee! Everything is monitored. A totally different approach to it.

Our love of the game wasn't any less than fellas' love of the game today. If that's what was there in our day, that's what we would have done. We were all terrible serious men and loved our county. We would give second to nobody, the same as the lads today.

It was different, we did what we were asked to do; we did what was necessary at the time.

Cork were way better than us in the Munster finals in 1982 and '83; there wasn't a whole lot we could do about that. We didn't play well on the day. I have a theory that you play as well as you're allowed play. You're not in control of a lot of things that happen in these games, because the other team is in control.

You try your heart out and you work your butt off, but we were never in either of the two Munster finals really. We never had a realistic chance.

Five minutes or 10 minutes into the match, it was gone from us. The worst moments of my inter-county career were those two moments, coming off that field. It was like someone died. It was hideous. You just wanted to hide but you couldn't.

You've got to take the kicks up the backside with the bouquets. They were hideous days, not just for me but for every one of us. We had a couple of great performances to get there but it just didn't materialise for us.

It was tremendous to win an All Star in 1982.

I had changed a lot of things in my life to get to that point and to achieve it in the end. They're supposed to ring you. They pick it on a night, ring you and ask you would you accept it before they announced it. That was the norm.

I was in for it a good few times. You're waiting and waiting.

You know that it's being picked, that these fellas are sitting down in a hotel in Dublin and they're picking the All Stars. You're waiting for the phone call... and you don't get it and that's it. It happened me a few times and this particular time it happened again.

I was waiting and I got no phone call.

I got up the next morning and I went into work in the glass factory at seven o'clock. Still no word. *That's it then, I didn't get it.*

I started up the bench and Lord have mercy on Larry Quinn, a Mount Sion man who was involved with underage in Waterford and the Tony Forristal tournament... he was in the factory and we were great friends. I was sitting down about ten past eight; I was a master glass cutter and I was firing into my job.

Next thing, Larry tapped me on the shoulder and I turned around and he said, 'Congratulations boy!'

'For what Larry? Don't mess me about, you could get a dig if you're codding me!'

'NO... NO!' he said. He had the paper with him, the *Independent*, and he showed it to me and I was an All Star. I took off my apron and went down and clocked out... and went off! I was gone in five minutes!

It was brilliant, sure. It was a life's ambition.

This was *yourself*, the dark winter nights training... on a diet in my case. If I looked at the kitchen, I'd put on weight! I had to control my diet through Christmas and all of a sudden this happens.

After being disappointed the year before and another couple of times and then, all of a sudden, it happened. It's the ultimate, personally… individually.

It will never be taken off me.

I was Waterford City's first All Star, Mount Sion's first All Star. I wasn't the first Waterford man but I was the first city man. A big honour.

I'm grateful to my family and to everybody. I worked hard for it. Joe McGrath came in and made a difference to me. There were different fellas that influenced me through that period and got me right. *Would I prefer a Munster medal?* Probably.

Would I prefer an All-Ireland medal? Definitely. As an individual, when other things are not possible, it was mega.

I was on the previous All Star trip as well; I was a replacement All Star. We went to New York and San Francisco the first time in 1981. The 1982 All Stars team went to New York, Los Angeles and San Francisco. We were gone nearly three weeks!

They were some trips in those days! Super trips like, top class. Now, they don't even play a match! We played two or three matches. The All-Ireland champions travelled with us. That's how you got replacement All Stars.

In 1981, Liam Fennelly was the All Star at left corner-forward. The All Stars were different in those days; there were three fellas nominated for left corner-forward in my case and one of us got it, and the other two got nothing. There was no such thing as putting me full-forward or right corner-forward.

In those days, three men were nominated for the position; one of them got it and one of the other two replaced him on the trip. Fennelly was playing with Kilkenny, who were the champions, so I replaced him on the All Star team.

We played a match every Sunday out there.

My father Paddy was on the Waterford team in 1938 for the All-Ireland, when Dublin beat them. He played for the county around that period. He was a founder member of the Mount Sion club in 1932… steeped in it.

The Munster medal was the Holy Grail. The funny thing about it is my father has a Munster medal and my son Brian has one, and I don't. I'm proud of them.

I'm proud of my father having one and I'm proud of my son having one. I never got it, the holy grail as we call it in the family.

I remember in Lawlors Hotel in 2002 when they came back to Dungarvan after winning it. I was up at the bar and Paul Flynn and Micheal White came up to me with the cup. One of them said to me, 'Hey, you're looking for this all your life aren't you!'

After the game, a fella wouldn't let me out on the field. I was over on the far side. The gate men weren't letting people in. I was saying, 'I have to go in. My son is out there... I need to go out there!'

He said, 'Sorry, nobody is going in there!'

'I'm not nobody!' I said. 'My son is out there.'

A few fellas were saying, 'That's Jim Greene...would you let him in!'

I was let in.

Myself and Fergal Hartley's father were sitting together at the match. Wonderful time. Liam, Fergal's brother, was there as well. We couldn't believe it. The two fathers were grand but I thought the young fella was going to get a heart attack!

It was one of the best days of my life. That was special, Brian's first senior medal. It was a feeling that I'd say fellas get when they get to the top of Mount Everest.

It was one of those moments. You couldn't explain it to anybody.

It was one of those things that you just can't put into words. It can't be imagined, it has to be lived. It's the Holy Grail. It's something you dream of... *Winning Munster*... your whole hurling life.

PAT McGRATH

The freedom of playing wing back, rather than in the centre, was something Pat McGrath always savoured (above, he is pictured with Kilkenny's Noel Skehan, Sligo's Mickey Kearins and Kerry's Mick O'Dwyer after being inducted into the GAA's Hall of Fame in 2014).

66

I ENDED UP being the loose man that afternoon in 1974, so I enjoyed that!

I was playing in the half-back line and Frankie Walsh and Seamus Power were in charge of the team. Frankie said to me, 'You go around the middle between the half-forward line and the half-backs... you clean up around that area'.

That's what I did and it worked out alright for me.

I liked playing left half-back. You could attack and you could go up the field. When you're centre-back, you're trying to hold the centre and you're going from side to side winning ball, but you're not really attacking much. At wing back, you could make a few solo runs up the field.

You had a little bit of freedom at left half-back, I thought.

There was a good atmosphere there because they had seats on the sideline in Walsh Park against the wall. There was a great atmosphere. Waterford weren't after winning many games. You played one game and if you were knocked out, you were gone. It was a great win for us.

The next day we were flying against Limerick in the first-half up in Thurles and we were up by 11 points. Actually, Tony Forristal said, 'We're going to have a bus now for the Munster final!'

My wife was with all of them in the stand. He thought we had the game won! We *thought* we had the game won, to be honest about it. They got three soft goals that got them back into the game and they won by a point. It would have been nice early in my career to have a win like that, to get to a Munster final. We hadn't a bad team then.

Martin Hickey doubled on a ball, and hit Mossie Walsh. Mossie was playing well. Mossie was centre-forward at that stage, if I'm not mistaken. Mossie had to go off, and that upset us a bit in the second-half.

We should have won that game. That's the way it goes, I suppose.

In my time, there was a lot more hitting to be honest about it. You had to sort a few fellas out at times. If someone hit you, that's it, you get him back. That's the way it was in the 70s. When the ball was up the field and a fella gave you a dunt, you gave it back to him.

You couldn't take it. You had to give it back to him. That's the way it was.

If you didn't stand up, a fella had you in his pocket… you know what I mean. You had to stand up and be counted.

In the 70s, we trained two days a week, Tuesdays and Thursdays in Dungarvan. An odd weekend you'd train. You wouldn't be killing yourself training. Before the championship, you'd be only training a month before a game. Not like they are now.

It wasn't as hectic as it is now. The club games were going on as well before the championship.

The first championship game I played was against Tipp; I was on Francis Loughnane. I thought he was a great player. Seamus Power said to me, 'You're on one of the top hurlers in Ireland'. This fella was top scorer… Francis Loughnane from Roscrea.

I wasn't even 18. I played well on him, I held him scoreless; he got a few points from frees, but at least I held him scoreless. I remember coming in at half-time and I was young and I thought I was fit, and my tongue was hanging.

Power was saying, 'You're getting the better of him, he's older than you… you have the legs on him'. But my tongue was hanging out trying to keep up with him!

Francis Loughnane was a complete left hander; he was hard to block. He was tough enough too, he was wiry; you had to be on top of your game to play against him. A few other fellas too. Pat Horgan used to play with Cork centre-forward and he was a big, tall lad and he was an awkward fella to play on.

I was living in Tycor Avenue; it's over those houses you can see from the stand in Walsh Park. Henry Moloney used to have the street leagues going and I used to play with Griffiths Place. 'Mull' Moloney used to be cutting the grass in Walsh Park.

At the time, they used to have sheep on the field eating the grass! To keep the grass down! I remember as a kid going over the wall into 'Mull' and playing on Walsh Park. We were eight or nine or 10… all young fellas. There used to be a gang of us that got over the wall and played in Walsh Park.

The street leagues were good for Waterford hurling, I thought. Some great players came from the street leagues. You had Roanmore, Morrisons Road, Griffiths Place… a team from Waterside and a team from Tramore. It taught a lot of people how to hurl. The matches would be up in Mount Sion or De La Salle or Poleberry; you'd get an odd game out in Tramore. Then, they used to pick a team out of the street leagues, the best 15, to go up to Dublin for a weekend and you would play St Vincent's and stay there for the weekend with a family.

They picked a few fellas from different teams to do that. It was a nice break.

We used to play hurling out on the streets in front of the Jute Factory. You'd have 12 fellas, maybe 14 fellas… seven-a-side playing hurling on the road. You'd be hitting the ball against the wall and learning the skills. There used to be a tennis place and you'd belt the ball off the back wall and the side wall.

That's how we learned.

Frankie Walsh, Powery, Martin Óg Morrissey and Larry Guinan were my heroes in Mount Sion. The fella in Waterford I really liked when I was very young was Tom Cheasty… *I loved Cheasty.*

My father was from Dunhill; he worked on Cheasty's farm years and years ago when he was young. He used to bring me to Walsh Park when I was young and Cheasty would be playing with Ballyduff and I loved the way he played. He got the ball between fellas and bust his way out. He was the fella I really enjoyed watching.

The first day I played against him was with the glass factory. He used to play with the farmers and I was centre-back and Cheasty was centre-forward. We had a bit of a battle. I was young enough at the time. After the game, he said, 'You're not a bad bit of stuff'. Coming from him, that was nice.

When I got a bit older, I liked Mick Roche from Tipperary; he used to play centre-back. I thought he was the complete hurler, a lovely striker, a fella who could read the game and win ball. I thought he was a very stylish hurler and I liked him.

I was surprised to enter the GAA Hall of Fame in 2014.

I thought it was only a joke at first! It was an honour for the family and the club. I was delighted with it. I remember going up to it and Noel Skehan was there; the last time I met Noel I was sent off after hitting him in a league game. I was up full-forward and Skehan was a fella for mouthing a bit in the goal.

I was on Dick O'Hara, who was full-back; the ball was going wide and he went to shield it to go wide. I went in and swiped at it and hit Skehan in the head. He hit the back of his head off the post so he was carried off and I was fired off!

That was near the end of my career when I was up full-forward!

A Cork man sent me a letter with 20 pounds in it! Cork were after playing Kilkenny in the All-Ireland that September and the league was just after that.

He'll be eating no more apples at an All-Ireland!' he wrote.

Someone threw an apple down the back of the goal in the All-Ireland and Kilkenny were winning, and Skehan started eating the apple that your man threw down!

So, I got a letter with 20 pounds and he goes… *Have a drink on me!'*

I thought this was very funny. We were training for the Munster club with Mount Sion, so I went up to the club and Pat Fanning was there and Jim Greene was there, and I said, 'Lads we can have a drink off of this after the game'.

Next thing, Fanning said, 'You can't do that. You can't be accepting money like that over hitting someone. We'll have to give that to charity'.

So, he took the 20 pounds off me and it went to charity! It was in the national papers.

Skehan retired after that, I think.

That was the first time I met him after, at the Hall of Fame, but we didn't mention it or anything like that!

99

JOHN GALVIN

WATERFORD 2-5 CLARE 1-3
Munster Under-21 HC Final
Semple Stadium
JULY 14, 1974

John Galvin (fourth from left in the back row in the 'Stars of the 80s' team presentation in Croke Park in 2013) has his under-21 days as his fondest memories in a Waterford shirt.

★ **WATERFORD:** W Ryan; F McCarthy, M Flynn, K Ryan; L O'Brien, **J Galvin**, E Ryan; P Egan, P McGrath (O-1); T Casey (O-3), L Power, P O'Keeffe; B Mansfield (O-1), M McNamara, P Moore (2-O).

★ **CLARE:** C Ryan; C McGuinness, S Stack, J Keogh; G Loughnane, S Hehir, J Ward; C Honan, J Callinan (1-O); J Treacy (O-1), J Bourke, P O'Connor (O-1); J Boyce, E O'Connor, M Gough. Subs: M McNamara (O-1) for Bourke, M McKeogh for Boyce.

THE ACTION

WATERFORD CAPTURED THEIR first Munster under-21 title as they turned over red-hot favourites Clare in a gripping provincial final on a rain-sodden Sunday evening.

The Banner enjoyed emphatic wins over Tipperary and Cork in the earlier rounds of the championship. They also boasted seven members of side that beat Tipperary in the senior semi-final seven days earlier, including Ger Loughnane. The Déise had easy victories against Limerick and Kerry.

John Galvin gave a masterclass at centre-back as the Waterford defence repelled the Banner. The Portlaw man was a tower of strength. He hurled minor, under-21 and senior in the same year and became the first Waterford man to pick up an All Star award in October. Captain Pat McGrath got the upper hand at midfield alongside Pat Egan. In the torrential rain, Waterford started brightly with a Brendan Mansfield free. They kept the ball moving on the wet surface. Pat O'Connor converted a free at the other end. Mansfield then turned provider for a Paul Moore goal on nine minutes. Clare goalkeeper Con Ryan made a marvellous save from Mossie McNamara. Pat McGrath, Tom Casey and Liam Power put over points to leave the Déise 1-4 to 0-2 ahead at the halfway stage.

Clare introduced Michael McNamara at full-forward and he pointed on the restart. Moore got his second goal 13 minutes from time, amid a goalmouth scramble, to kill off the Clare challenge. Tom Casey tagged on a point from a free. John Callinan drilled home a consolation goal for Clare from a 21-yard free.

A first provincial crown at any grade for the Déise since the senior success of 1963 and a first underage title since 1948. Waterford beat Antrim comfortably in the All-Ireland semi final (3-18 to 1-2), but they lost a thrilling final to Kilkenny by a single point in Thurles (3-8 to 3-7).

★★★★★

66

I'M GOING TO take you back a long ways. I'm going to take you back to 1974.

We had a good under-21 team. We played Limerick in the first round and we beat them decisively; we played Kerry and, then, in the Munster final Clare had a star-studded team with Ger Loughnane, the O'Connors and Sean Stack. It was played on a Sunday night in Thurles, on the day of the Munster football final.

Clare were raging hot favourites and all the papers had written us off. We went up to Thurles and nobody gave us a chance except ourselves.

Our team was made up of lads from Fourmilewater, Cappoquin, Tallow, Mount Sion, Ballydurn, Ballyduff Upper, Ferrybank... we had a cross-section from the whole county. It was a team that gelled together and got on very well. On the night, we played absolutely out of our skins. I played centre-back.

I started off actually in goal. I played a challenge match for Waterford in goal at minor. When it came to the championship, I was very young so I didn't play in the goal. At that time, the minor and the senior games were played on the one day; the minor before the senior. I was picked on the senior team... and I was picked on the minor team. The minor match was postponed to the following Wednesday night so that I could play centrefield on the senior team; centrefield against Cork down in the Athletic Grounds.

When I was at the peak of my powers, I loved playing centre-back. I always say to someone that it's the best position on the field because it's the one position where you have the most influence on the game. A good centre-back, like Tadhg De Búrca... he can control the game from where he is at centre-back. You're looking up the field and you can put that ball where you want to put it.

It's the best position on the field for hurling.

I was marking Enda O'Connor in the Munster final. That was a great night now. That team was after making a breakthrough. The only pity was that more fellas off that team didn't go on to play senior.

My style was totally hurling. Playing the ball.

Even when I played full-back, I never played the game as a stopper, we'll say. I always tried to hurl the ball all the time which probably didn't work at times. That was the way I played; I didn't know any other way of playing.

That 1974 team, we went on then and we played Antrim in Belfast. You can imagine in '74, it was the height of the Troubles; things weren't too rosy up in Belfast at that time. I can remember we were in Dublin and we got the train to Belfast and when we arrived in Victoria Station, the station was there but there was no roof… there was nothing on it, it was after being blown off it.

We had an armed guard from the station up to the game, and the same on the way back. Onto the train… and straight back down again after the match. We had beaten Antrim and beaten them comprehensively.

We played Kilkenny then in the final and they had Brian Cody, Joe Hennessy, Billy Fitzpatrick, Ger Fennelly… *all those men*. They had a star-studded team. They beat us 3-8 to 3-7 in the final. We were so close.

That game in Thurles was a marvellous game, we were really unlucky. We got caught for a soft goal and that's what beat us. We had exceptional forwards on that team; we had Tom Casey from Dunhill, Mossie McNamara from Ballyduff Upper, Paul Moore from Ferrybank and Brendan Mansfield from Ballydurn.

Pat McGrath from Mount Sion was centrefield and then we had Micheal Flynn from Abbeyside full-back. We had a mix from all over the county… it was an exceptional team.

Later in 1974, I was picked on the All Star team. At that time, the All Star team was announced in the paper on a Monday morning. I remember the Sunday night; I was at home in my own house with my mother.

My father and Pat Coffey – Paudie Coffey's father – always went out for a drink on a Sunday night. Seán Óg Ó Ceallacháin, who did the GAA results on the radio on a Sunday night, he got an inkling of the team so he rang Seamus Grant… and Seamus Grant rang Pat Coffey.

The two lads came down from the pub and came into the house… that's the way I found out. It was announced then the following morning.

It was hard to believe it. I was after playing senior for Waterford and I was after playing under-21 for Waterford and minor; I played both codes, football and hurling. It was incredible. I didn't expect it. It was the furthest thing from my mind at the time. For the club and for the county, it was a massive boost.

The first All Star trip was with Carrolls as sponsors. When you went out that time, you stayed with families. All the players were with families. I roomed with the famous Down footballer Colm McAlarney. We were great friends after. I roomed with him and we had a great time. We were in Los Angeles, San Francisco and then back to New York.

I was only 20 at the time, so coming straight from Portlaw... not being anywhere outside the country, to be landed in the middle of Los Angeles! I tell you it was an eye-opener!

They were great trips. The 1982 trip was an especially great trip.

I'd have a big grá for gaelic football and I was lucky enough I got very friendly with the great Kerry team at the time. To the present day, I'd be very friendly with Mikey Sheehy. I knocked around with them when I was out there. They're the things that you remember about the trips; the men you met.

The Dublin team at the time was starting to show their teeth. Eoin Liston and Páidí Ó Sé... meeting up with those lads and meeting up with the hurling fellas, that was the major plus of the trip. All the fellas you played against... finally meeting them and socialising with them.

The first day I played in the National Hurling League for Waterford, it was against Kilkenny in Nowlan Park. It was a baptism of fire because I was centrefield on the team and I was playing on probably the best centrefield player that ever played with Kilkenny... Paddy Moran. He was an exceptional hurler.

That day Waterford FC were playing Cork Celtic down in Flower Lodge and I was picked to play centre-half that day for Waterford too. So, I had a decision to make.

My father was probably the biggest influence on my career because he won an All-Ireland medal in 1948; he was corner-forward on that team. He said to me, 'Look, it's your decision, if you play soccer, you play soccer... if you play hurling, you play hurling. Whatever you play, it's your decision'.

I remember Pat Coffey, who was selector with Waterford at the time, came over and said to me, 'What are you going to do?' I decided that I was going to go to Kilkenny to play hurling for Waterford, and I never regretted it.

I opted for the GAA and I *never* regretted it.

We had no silverware to show for it but I enjoyed every minute I put on that county jersey. I got a lot out of it because I got two All Star trips, and I played for the Rest of Ireland and I played for Munster, so that made up for everything. I never regretted making that decision anyway.

It was like a religion in the house.

When I was growing up, my father was involved in the Portlaw club, and as you could imagine, the whole way up I was going to matches. It was bred into us. He had seven brothers and James, my uncle, was on the 1948 team as well. I believe when he was hurling himself, he relied on his hurling all the time. He always impressed upon me that the ball was the most important thing on the field... and nothing else counted.

I always regret that we didn't make the big breakthrough with Waterford. We came close a few times and we had some good teams. In 1982 and '83, we got the mother and father of a beating off Cork. That wasn't the true team, we didn't perform.

It was a big thing at that time for us to make the final in 1982. *Whether it was the occasion or whatever?* I can always remember that day in Thurles; you couldn't hear your ears with the noise. At that time, the crowd were nearer to the pitch than what they are now. That was one of the biggest regrets that I didn't win a Munster medal or an All-Ireland medal.

In saying that, looking back on it, I wouldn't have done anything different. I enjoyed every single minute that I played.

Myself and Roseann were married in 1978. We were married on a Saturday and Waterford played the quarter-finals of the National League on the Sunday; and I played full-back against Wexford and Tony Doran. That was a baptism... the day after our wedding!

As regards hurling ability and everything like that, there were two fellas. Jimmy Barry-Murphy was definitely one of them, and Billy Fitzpatrick was another fella from Kilkenny. They were two stylists and two complete stickmen.

They were two great players and I always enjoyed playing against them. It mightn't have always worked out the best against them but I always enjoyed playing against them.

SEAMIE HANNON

WATERFORD 4-13 TIPPERARY 2-15
Munster SHC Semi-Final
Páirc Uí Chaoimh
JUNE 19, 1983

Seamie Hannon believes that the treatment of Justin McCarthy by the Waterford players was unpardonable (above, Seamie is photographed in 2005 with McCarthy and Nicky Cashin).

★ **WATERFORD:** J Power; K Ryan, J Galvin, **S Hannon**; C Curley, P McGrath (0-2), P Ryan (0-2); M Walsh (0-2), E Nolan; E Rockett (1-1), S Breen (1-0), T Maher; T Casey (1-3), P Bennett, J Greene (1-2). Subs: J Hennebry (0-1) for Nolan, L O'Brien for Galvin, K Delahunty for Bennett.

★ **TIPPERARY:** J Sheedy; Eddie Hogan, P Brennan, Enda Hogan; P Fitzelle (0-3), J McIntyre, B Ryan; L Bergin, R Callaghan (1-0); M Doyle (0-1), L Maher (0-2), P Dooley (0-1); T Waters (1-1), J Grogan (0-6), N English (0-1). Subs: T Stapleton for McIntyre, P McGrath for Eddie Hogan, S Burke for Dooley.

THE ACTION

WATERFORD FOUGHT BACK from six points down to make it back to the Munster final after a fiery encounter with Tipperary. In sweltering conditions, Jim Greene got the vital goal with 12 minutes to go. Kieran Ryan, Pat McGrath, Mossie Walsh, Tom Casey, Greene and Eddie Rockett were the main men in front of a crowd of 15,450. Corner-back Seamie Hannon captained the side after Ballyduff Upper captured their first county title in 1982.

Déise corner-forward Tom Casey rattled the back of the net after two minutes. Tipp levelled by the 10th minute before Ralph Callaghan's shot slipped through the fingers of Waterford goalkeeper John Power. Stephen Breen goaled on 22 minutes after he beat Tipp goalkeeper John Sheedy to a ground ball. Tipp went in 1-10 to 2-4 ahead at the break.

A minute into the second period, the Premier County extended that lead to six as Tommy Waters hit in a low shot which flew in off John Galvin's hurley. At the other end, Sheedy saved from Tom Casey, but Eddie Rockett blasted home the rebound.

Liam O'Brien replaced John Galvin, who only recently recovered from illness, and Kieran Ryan moved to full-back. The switch proved to be a masterstroke as Ryan got to grips with Tipp full-forward John Grogan.

Grogan had a glorious chance of a goal but hit the ball into the ground. The Déise took the lead when Greene hit the net on 58 minutes. Sub Jim Hennebry then landed a long-distance point. Grogan dispatched two frees to leave just one between them.

Mossie Walsh got on top at midfield. The Ballyduff Upper man grabbed a puck-out from John Power and sent the ball between the posts. Walsh added another long range effort before Greene sealed victory.

★★★★★

"

I remember the game was a fairly needly affair and in the aftermath the Tipp fans and the Tipp players were very critical of the referee, implying he was lenient on a very physical Waterford team.

I was cautioned twice and my clubmate Mossie Walsh was cautioned three times. Both would be red cards in today's game!

I played in my usual left corner-back position and was marking Tommy Waters. He was substituted during the game; I then marked Michael Doyle. Doyle was a bit of a handful as he was speedy and good at running into space.

Being a defender, at that time, the order of the day was that if you were second to the ball, you were last. It was straightforward after that, you were going forward and getting the ball out the field as quickly as possible. No back-passes or passes across the goal back then. Get the ball to where it was most beneficial was the instruction.

Ballyduff Upper won the county championship for the first time in 1982 so I was Waterford captain in '83. Myself and Mossie Walsh tossed for it in the local pub! I won the toss, that's how I became captain in '83! Mossie was our main man in the club at that time. He was a garda and while he was stationed in Ballyshannon in Donegal, he drove back to Ballyduff for training and games.

Near the end of the game, I was clearing a ball when Tipp forward Nicky English lunged in to intercept it. I pulled and got Nicky straight into the face and mouth full whack with the hurley. He had a really nasty facial injury and anyone who has read his book with Vincent Hogan called *Beyond The Tunnel* will be aware of the extent of those injuries.

Tipp had used all their subs and I remember their selector roaring at Nicky to get up as he approached him on the field. He looked down at him and said, 'Jesus Christ, you're destroyed!'

He was taken to hospital and had surgery on his face. Thankfully, it didn't damage his hurling career and he played many excellent games for Tipp after that.

In February 1983, we played Kilkenny in a National League game in Nowlan Park and I got a very serious shoulder injury. I got sandwiched between Billy Fitzpatrick and one of the Fennellys. I was taken to the local hospital but got transferred to Cork as I needed surgery. I spent a week in hospital and several weeks with my shoulder immobilised; I had four pins inserted into it. I was supposed to be out for up to 12 months but… here I was leading out Waterford in June.

The build-up to the 1983 Munster final was similar to '82 despite the hammering we got from Cork that year. My mother was a Cork woman and one of my farms is on the Cork border with just a stream dividing the two counties, so you can imagine the banter was unbelievable. Again, we were well beaten by a great Cork team who amazingly were still finding it difficult to beat Kilkenny.

Losing two Munster finals in-a-row was hard to take and there were days out on the farm when I wondered was it worth all the effort… *would I stay or go?* I eventually stayed on for a few more years but, again, no trophies.

While I played for Waterford, starting as a minor on both the football and hurling teams, my total winnings were a Railway Cup medal in 1976, a Division Two National League… and I was an All Star replacement in 1975. That was a memorable trip for several reasons. I broke my ankle a few days before we travelled out. I couldn't play so I commentated on the games. Kilkenny were All-Ireland champions and I was paired with Fan Larkin and the late Georgie Leahy.

I was selector with Joe McGrath during his time with Waterford and later with Justin McCarthy when success finally came our way. It was an honour to serve as a selector with Justin during that period and my only regret is how shabbily he was treated after bringing so much success and enjoyment to the people of Waterford.

Justin had a long association with Ballyduff Upper, as his aunt was married to the local garda sergeant and they lived in the Ballyduff barracks. Justin used to come on holidays as a young lad. Pity he didn't move down here and play with us!

Overall, a lean trophy cabinet, but lots of good and not so good memories. However, the good outweigh the bad and I was always proud to wear a Waterford jersey and none more so than leading them out against Tipp in Páirc Uí Chaoimh on June 19, 1983.

MOSSIE WALSH

WATERFORD 3-10 CORK 1-16
National Hurling League
Walsh Park
MARCH 27, 1983

Mossie Walsh (fourth from the left in the back row) knew Waterford needed a big performance against Cork in the spring of 1983 if they were to have any championship ambitions that year.

★ **WATERFORD:** J Power; K Ryan, J Galvin, L O'Brien; C Curley, P McGrath, P Ryan; **Mossie Walsh (0-1)**, R Walsh; K Delahunty, T Maher, S Breen (1-1); Michael Walsh (1-7), P Bennett (1-1), J Greene. Sub: E Nolan for R Walsh.

★ **CORK:** G Cunningham; S O'Gorman, J Crowley, B Murphy; T Cashman (0-1), P Horgan (0-2), D McCurtain; T McCarthy, M Lyons (0-1); B Óg Murphy (0-5), T Crowley, J Barry-Murphy (1-1); P Crowley (0-1), K Hennessy (0-1), J Buckley (0-3). Subs: D Walsh (0-1) for T Crowley, F Collins for McCarthy.

THE ACTION

WATERFORD RALLIED FROM nine points down to grab a share of the spoils with Cork and stay up in Division One of the National Hurling League. In front of 3,000 fans at Walsh Park, a 60-yard free in the dying seconds from Michael Walsh retained their status in the top flight.

Eight months earlier, the Rebels routed the Déise by 31 points in the Munster final (5-31 to 3-6). An embarrassing afternoon for Waterford hurling.

Brothers Mossie (an All Star midfielder in 1980), Richie and Michael Walsh from Ballyduff Upper all started for the home side. The Reds won their first Waterford Senior Championship in 1982.

Another one-sided contest was on the cards when the visitors went in 1-12 to 1-3 to the good at the break. Waterford's first point came from a Michael Walsh free after 16 minutes. Mossie Walsh then got the ball into Pat Bennett and he buried it into the back of the Cork net. Jimmy Barry-Murphy raised a green flag at the other end a minute before the interval.

Two goals in as many minutes from Michael Walsh and Stephen Breen on the restart turned this match on its head... 1-12 to 3-3. Game on.

It took Cork 14 minutes to get their first score of the second-half through John Buckley. Michael Walsh joined his brother Mossie at midfield as Waterford reeled in their opponents point by point. Michael kept tapping over the placed balls, and Pat Bennett was accurate from play.

Bertie Óg Murphy gave Cork a two-point advantage with time ticking down. Waterford weren't finished yet as Michael Walsh made it a one-point game. Their main marksman then held his nerve with that late, long-range free to level the scores, bringing his total to 1-7 and keeping Waterford in Division One.

Pride restored after that Munster final massacre.

★★★★★

"

AFTER GETTING HAMMERED by Cork in the Munster final in 1982, this game meant a lot. It was our first time meeting them again. I know it was only the league, but I felt that we had to play well.

Had we lost that game, we were gone into Division Two. Prior to Christmas, we played Offaly and we beat them in Dungarvan but we lost subsequent games to Kilkenny and Galway. This was a relegation battle for us. We played exceptionally well on the day.

Also, the three Walshs were playing in that one…. myself, Michael and Richie. Richie and myself were in midfield and Michael was in the full-forward line.

When we were younger, on Sunday mornings after Mass, we'd be flaking the ball up and down the road. There wasn't much traffic! We were at it all the time.

Michael was much younger than myself, but he was the most talented of us. He won Fitzgibbon Cups and everything with UCC. He was a class hurler. He finished up early because he had a back injury, but he was the class act in the family. The rest of us were about pure effort and staying at it, as the fella says.

I wouldn't have had the class of the vast majority of hurlers, but I brought pure determination and effort. I played most games at midfield which suited me. A bit of room there. At that time, there was a lot more ball being played in the middle of the field. The ball wasn't travelling over into the '21' at that stage.

You got your rewards by putting in the effort.

I can tell you, it was always an ambition to play in a Munster final but you'd be saying to yourself… *15 men against 15 men… how could we get such a hammering?* We were definitely dejected after 1982, there's no doubt about that.

You have to pull yourself together. Following on from the league, we beat Tipperary in the first round of the Munster Championship in Cork in 1983. That brought us to another Munster final against Cork, which wasn't much better!

You'd always get that vibe from the near neighbours. There was always rivalry there. To get such a beating, it was unbelievable, there was no doubt about that.

I played on Tim Crowley, and John Fenton was in the middle of the field the same day. Tim said to me at one stage, 'You'd hope that the ground would open up'. In a nice way like. We were so low at that stage.

It was hard to comprehend it really. We trained very hard and everything. Once we went on the field again with them, in the league, we needed to play well.

I was in Limerick for eight or nine years with the Gardai and over the winter period I'd come down twice a week for training to Dungarvan. I felt myself at that stage that if I didn't stick at it, I could be dropped. I wasn't going to give them that opportunity!

I didn't mind it at that stage; I enjoyed doing what I was doing.

I must say that Joe McGrath was a very professional man in those days, there's no doubt about that. He was top class. It was methodical. He had everything set out. Before you started, you knew what you were doing. Time was time. He was certainly way ahead of *his* time, there's no doubt about that.

Unfortunately, at that time, you got one chance and that was it. It was in or out. It's a totally different system now. We had more one-day outings than anything at that stage with the county.

The All Star in 1980 was unbelievable.

It's the next best thing to an All-Ireland, if you can't get that far. It was enormous for the club, Ballyduff Upper… a small little rural club. It doesn't happen too often. It happens more often now with the success the county are having. Back at that stage, it was certainly big.

I was in Tramore at that stage. The Bank of Ireland were sponsoring the All Stars; it was actually the manager of the Bank of Ireland in Waterford who contacted me. That's how I became aware of that.

I got a replacement All Star in 1979 and, I suppose, I was still performing fairly well so that's the way it came. You were selected in the position you played in at that time. That has changed. Now, you can be selected in a position that you haven't played that often.

You get out of it what you put into it. It's as simple as that.

I know myself, I used to leave Limerick in the winter evenings at half past five and it could be half eleven or twelve o'clock when I'd get back, you know. It wasn't an issue. I was young at the time and I did it because I enjoyed it.

For the All Star trip, we went to New York and Boston, and to San Francisco as well. They were terrific altogether. Galway were All-Ireland champions at that stage so we travelled with them, and Kerry were All-Ireland champions in the football. It was a terrific trip, there's no doubt about it.

The amazing thing about it, all those lads with All Ireland medals and All Stars and everything, they were so ordinary; they were a pleasure to be with, they were top class.

John Connolly of Galway was a star midfielder. There's no doubt about it. A top class hurler. But the toughest man of all that I came across was Frank Cummins of Kilkenny. We played them in a league semi-final in 1982; we drew with them and they beat us in the replay. Frank was a mighty, well built man.

I was light enough myself but I went to take him on with a shoulder above in Thurles and he shifted me back four or five yards with his strength! He was a physical man, strong and well built. Not a dirty hurler by any means, but you'd know that you were playing against him, I can assure you!

I nearly lost the top portion of my lip in a garda match down in the Mount Sion pitch, a challenge match against Mount Sion. I was very lucky that there was a great surgeon in Ardkeen. It was only hanging on as such. I lost most of my teeth, but you get over these things. It's all part and parcel of it.

It was just a pure accident. I slipped and my hurley went at an angle and the other player's hurley flew up and hit me in the mouth. I had a bad facial injury at that time alright.

At that stage, the helmets started to come in.

It was Paddy Crowley in Cork – he would be a brother of Tim's… he is a doctor and he produced the first helmets, I think. I remember going to RTÉ to do an interview about these helmets. Since then, they have improved every aspect of the helmets.

They were a monstrosity of a thing, the first ones that came out, until they refined them. I was one of the first to wear a helmet… a long time ago now!

LIAM O'CONNOR

WATERFORD 4-10 GALWAY 3-10
National Hurling League
Fraher Field
FEBRUARY 21, 1988

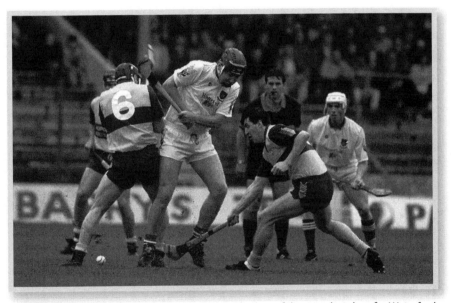

Ending Galway's unbeaten run of 15-months remains one of the proudest days for Waterford dual star Liam O'Connor (above, battling with Clare in Semple Stadium in 1992).

★ **WATERFORD:** P Curran; P Walsh, D Byrne, D Foran; J Beresford, **L O'Connor**, T Sheehan; N Crowley (0-1), B Power; K Delahunty (0-6), S Ahearne (1-2), M Neville; B O'Sullivan, J McDonald (2-0), M Walsh (0-1). Sub: P Bennett (1-0) for Neville.

★ **GALWAY:** J Commins (1-0); S Linnane, C Hayes, O Kilkenny; T Keady (0-1), P Piggott, M Monaghan; S Mahon, P Malone; M McGrath, J Cooney (0-6), M Naughton (0-1); E Ryan (1-1), B Lynskey (1-1), A Cunningham. Subs: T Kilkenny for Mahon, P Nolan for Malone.

THE ACTION

GALWAY'S 15-MONTH UNBEATEN record came to an end in Dungarvan as Waterford defeated the reigning All-Ireland, league and Railway Cup champions in a fiery encounter. A giant-killing for Tony Mansfield's team, who only emerged from Division Two the year before. When the two sides met in the league semi-final the previous April, the Tribesmen triumphed by 16 points at O'Moore Park (5-16 to 1-12). Revenge was sweet.

Noel Crowley lorded the midfield exchanges for the home side over the hour. Liam 'Chuck' O'Connor was first choice centre-back for three seasons at this stage and had All Star forward Joe Cooney for company on this occasion.

In the sixth minute, Shane Ahearne grabbed a sideline cut from Crowley and rattled the Galway net. Full-forward John McDonald booted home a second goal. Déise captain Michael Walsh chipped in with a point, while Crowley sent over a '65'.

Brendan Lynskey netted at the other end and set up another goal for Eanna Ryan as the Westerners went 2-5 to 2-2 ahead. Four points from Waterford free-taker Kieran Delahunty and one from Ahearne sent the Déise 2-7 to 2-5 up at the break.

McDonald crashed home his second goal and Waterford's third five minutes into the second-half. Crowley and McDonald then set up substitute Pat Bennett for another goal as the hosts opened up a two-goal advantage (4-8 to 2-8). Galway didn't give up, as Joe Cooney and Tony Keady pointed. With four minutes left, goalkeeper John Commins ran the length of the field and rifled a close range free to the net. One point in it. The game was on a knife-edge. Spurred on by the home support, Delahunty dispatched another free before Ahearne added a point from play. In a dramatic finish, Bennett broke through but Commins saved his goalbound effort.

★ ★ ★ ★ ★

66

IN 1984, I MADE my debut against Roscommon. If someone said to you, Waterford are playing Roscommon in the National Hurling League, you'd say that would be a 20-point win for Waterford. We were actually beaten the same day.

It was a very inauspicious start to my career. I was also on a team that was beaten by Mayo, and on a championship team beaten by Kerry. The low points were there.

Tony Mansfield probably didn't get as much credit as the man deserved. A terrific organiser, a brilliant man to motivate a team in the dressing-room. We never trained as hard we did in the winter of 1987. We realised coming up from Division Two that we had to get the fitness levels up.

Also, there were some tremendous hurlers on that team. You had Shane 'Shiner' Ahearne, Damian Byrne... Kieran Delahunty was a supreme free-taker, Noelie Crowley was probably something akin to Jamie Barron in the sense that he was a human dynamo... he ran box-to-box. We had Jimmy Beresford, Daithí Foran, Timmy Sheehan... outstanding hurlers. They were all leaders.

They all wanted to do what had to be done to better themselves as hurlers. Mansfield put a bit of pride back into Waterford.

I was always of the opinion that no matter who we were playing, we were always good enough to beat them. Unfortunately, we probably didn't have enough players of that mindset. The structures weren't anywhere near as professional as they should have been. In fairness to Tony, he had Ollie Wilkinson from Tourin and Phil Fanning from Mount Sion, they were the management committee.

Tony was a brilliant man-manager and a brilliant motivator. In 2013, Tony died and to a man, every one of that squad from 1987 up to '90 or '91 were at that man's funeral. They had the height of respect Tony.

The main effect of that win over Galway was that it restored pride into a very proud hurling county. It gave us a bit of confidence and a bit of belief that we could beat the best. That team went on to beat Cork in the replay of the Munster semi-final, which we had never done.

We had slipped so far. Everybody talks about the demise of Offaly hurling; Waterford hurling fell further from grace back then. That was terrible for a county with a proud tradition and a history of winning All-Irelands. It was important to get back to the top table and we did that.

We were unfortunate enough at the time to run into a very strong Tipp team – we could never manage them in the league semi-final up in Croke Park and the Munster final in 1989.

Galway were *the* team then. You must remember Galway were unbeaten in league, Oireachtas and championship for 15 months up to that. We beat them in a fairly physical match in Fraher Field.

John McDonald from Kilkenny played in that game and he scored two goals. He was marking Sylvie Linnane. He played championship with Kilkenny in 1989, but he hurled with Waterford in '87 and '88.

The game was quite physical and bordering on dirty. Sylvie Linnane shipped a belt from McDonald; I believe it was a loose hurl more than intentional. Sylvie never wore a helmet… went back on the field of play with a bandage on his head and played like a man possessed for the remainder of the match.

With five or six minutes to go, McDonald was trying to make peace with Sylvie and said, 'There can't be many more minutes left, Sylvie'.

Sylvie, I'm told, turned around and said, 'Long enough for you, my friend!'

Lo and behold, the ball was down in our full-back line and the next thing, all I saw was McDonald panned out on the ground.

We beat Cork away, Kilkenny at home, Limerick away and Clare away in that league campaign. It was a big step-up for us coming from Division Two hurling. It gave the group great confidence. That Galway team was something similar to the current Limerick team; a big, strong physical team with fast, lively inside forwards.

I was at centre-back marking Joe Cooney and from time to time Brendan Lynskey used to come out on me. They were like chalk and cheese. Joe Cooney was the complete hurler. Brendan Lynskey was a physical player; he wasn't dirty but you'd know you were after marking him.

I broke a bone in my foot in the latter part of the league in 1989. I actually missed the first match against Cork; I came on in the last 10 minutes and started the replay. By that stage, I was moved up to centre-forward or full-forward. I actually played midfield against Kerry in 1993. Centre-back was my favourite position.

It was a handy enough position to play at that time. I was quite tall and imposing, and I was good under a high ball. Being from a football background was a help. In 1988, I was 22 so I was quite young. Then, I moved up the field and I finished up the remainder of the matches for Waterford in the forwards. That back-line... we had Jimmy Beresford on one wing and Timmy Sheehan on the other wing. A full-back line of Peter Walsh, Damian Byrne and Daithí Foran... and then you had Pat Curran in the goal.

We had good characters there.

My family were Erins Own.

My uncle would have played on the 1948 team... Kevin O'Connor, in Waterford's first All-Ireland. My uncle Paddy O'Connor was masseur with the Waterford team in the 70s and 80s, and chairman of Erins Own.

I went to school in St Declan's in Waterford City; St Declan's was one of the feeder schools for De La Salle. But at the time, there was more of a tradition in St Declan's of playing gaelic football.

I was a more natural footballer. I played football from age five or six; I only started playing hurling when I was 10 or 11. If you asked anyone about me, they'd say I was a manufactured hurler and a natural footballer.

I have some fantastic memories playing under Alo Curran, who was managing the Waterford football team at the time. Now, with the modern dual player, it's nearly impossible because you're trying to serve both masters. To be fair, three years in-a-row... 1986, '87 and '88, I played both football and hurling with Waterford. The reason I was able to do it was the great communication between Tony Mansfield and Alo Curran. There was a stage where I literally trained with the footballers one week, and trained with the hurlers the following week.

Nobody wants to be training hard all the time, they want to play matches. That was ideal; I was going from match to match. If they thought you were doing too much, they were clever to let you sit it out or just take it easy.

Standing for the national anthem is one of the best feelings you can have as a player. It's indescribable. The first time I pulled on the Waterford jersey, the hairs stood on the back of my neck because not alone are you representing yourself, you are representing your club, your family... your county.

That's tremendous, to have the honour of wearing the jersey. It's an honour that falls to very, very few. For me, it was an absolute privilege to wear the jersey in hurling and in football. After I retired, I felt it was important to give something back. I got involved with the development squads, the Tony Forristal in 2007 and then I was with the minor team all the way through to 2011. You only have the one county and that's *your* county.

I moved to Kilkenny with work. I worked with Woodchester Finance and at the time we didn't have a presence in Kilkenny and I was asked to move up. The first year I actually hurled away with my club Erins Own. We were intermediate and we were beaten in a few county finals. To help from a business point of view, I moved to James Stephens in Kilkenny and it worked out well for me.

I continued to play with the Village for 13 or 14 years, until I finished in 2003. Maybe they were waiting for me to finish because they won the club championship in 2004 and the club All-Ireland in 2005!

I never thought about transferring to Kilkenny. Brian Cody was our club manager at the time and Ollie Walsh was the Kilkenny manager in the early 90s. I remember at one stage during a club campaign we were training in Larchfield one night. There wasn't a direct approach but Brian said to me, 'Would you be contemplating wearing the stripes?'

I looked at him.

'What do you think?'

He said, 'Probably not.'

'No!'

When I was involved with underage teams in the Village, the development squads in Kilkenny had a good operation and they approached me. I said no.

'What do you want me to do? Train young Kilkenny lads to beat young Waterford lads?'

The opportunity came to get involved with the development squads in Waterford, so I was happy to do that.

DAMIAN BYRNE
(& SHANE AHEARNE)

WATERFORD 5-16 CORK 4-17
Munster SHC Semi-Final Replay
Semple Stadium
JUNE 18, 1989

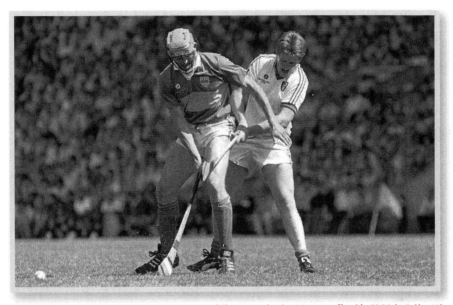

Damian Byrne challenges Cormac Bonnar of Tipperary in the Munster final in 1989 in Páirc Uí Chaoimh.

★ **WATERFORD:** J Power; P Walsh, **D Byrne**, S Prendergast; J Beresford, G Fitzpatrick, T Sheehan; N Crowley (0-6), P Prendergast; A Qualter (0-3), S Ahearne (1-3), K Delahunty (0-1); B O'Sullivan (1-2), L O'Connor (0-1), G Connors. Subs: P Murphy (3-0) for Connors, M Walsh for P Prendergast, S Cullinane for M Walsh.

★ **CORK:** G Cunningham; D Mulcahy, R Browne, W Cashman; J O'Connor, D Walsh, D Irwin; P O'Connor, J Cashman; M Mullins (0-1), T McCarthy (1-1), T O'Sullivan (0-1); M Foley (2-0), S O'Gorman (0-3), F Delaney (1-11). Subs: C Casey for W Cashman, K Kingston for J O'Connor, B Cunningham for Mullins.

THE ACTION

A SECOND-HALF HAT-TRICK from super-sub Pat Murphy saw Waterford claim their first win over Cork since 1974 and set up a Munster final with Tipperary. Unchartered territory.

A first Munster final appearance in six years after a nine-goal thriller. Midfielder Noelie Crowley, full-back Damian Byrne, centre-back Ger Fitzpatrick and captain Shane Ahearne were among the Déise heroes.

Waterford surrendered a six-point lead two weeks previously as the Rebels came back to earn a replay (18 points each). Cork led 3-11 to 2-10 at the break in the rematch with two goals from Mark Foley and one from Teddy McCarthy. Billy O'Sullivan netted early for Waterford as they went four points up after two minutes, but Cork turned it around to move six points clear.

Man of the Match Crowley landed three points in response before an attempted clearance from Cork keeper Ger Cunningham went in off Ahearne.

For the second-half, Ahearne moved out to midfield; O'Connor went to centre-forward, and Pat Murphy was introduced on the edge of the square. On the resumption, Murphy goaled with his first touch of the game and O'Sullivan added two points. Crowley gave a tour de force and shot six points in total.

A Finbarr Delaney goal edged Cork back in front. Cunningham was injured as he tried to prevent Waterford fourth's goal. He lost the flight of a delivery from Pat Ryan, the ball struck the crossbar and Murphy finished it off. Another Cunningham mistake allowed the Tallow man to complete his hat-trick. Cork nearly forced extra-time as Sean O'Gorman blasted a shot over the bar in the last minute.

Waterford had a price to pay for their success however as the Munster Council hit the county board with a £600 fine for incursions onto the field by team mentors and water carriers. More controversy was to follow in a tempestuous final clash with Tipperary.

★★★★★

66

I *LOVED* EVERYTHING about hurling, I still do.

I love everything about it; the skill levels, the way they're prepared now, the athleticism, though the physicality is going out of it a small bit.

I loved playing, I loved every minute of it. I'd *love* to be still doing it.

Tony Mansfield made men out of us. I had great time for him. He was a direct man and he was honest. He was a real Waterford man to the backbone, though he was having to battle against the hierarchy at the time. It took two Cork men to come along for our hierarchy to realise what it took to win matches in my opinion. Tony was always trying to prepare the team as best he could with his hands tied behind his back, if you know what I mean.

Everyone expected Cork to win. We had a fairly decent team at the time, I thought. Cork probably underestimated us, they probably said that they would beat us in the replay. Tony did a great job on us mentally for the replay because at that time Cork were beating Waterford every chance they got.

Any time you win a championship match you're bound to get confidence. I was an intermediate hurler for most of my club days. When you win a few matches, it gives great confidence to everyone. You go out in May or June and you're beaten and 'Good luck'… which is the way it was, you can't complain about it.

It would have been lovely to get a backdoor situation. Also, the preparation of teams at the moment is brilliant for players.

I always thought that our County Board at the time hadn't enough ambition. *Very negative*, I thought. It was frustrating for every player even before my time, I'd imagine. Just the treatment after training, and the amateurness of our set-up, compared to Tipperary and Cork. I always said that the fellas playing football for the county must have really loved the game because they were probably treated desperate altogether. We were a long way behind in terms of professionalism.

I remember being a selector in 2001 with Colm Bonnar, when Gerald McCarthy was manager. We'd be travelling to matches and I'd be comparing stories with him. They were light years ahead of us… light years as regards preparation and small things, but they all add up.

We probably had a decent enough team. I'm not solely blaming the County Board. Maybe we weren't good enough. Maybe I have rose-tinted glasses on me. But I would say that there was probably more in that team from that era.

Look, that's the way it was at the time. It was no individual's fault. You see how quickly things changed when the Cork lads came in and showed everybody, players and officials, what it took if they wanted to compete at the top table.

I was very young starting out with Waterford; I was at the tail-end of the last team that was in a Munster final in 1983. They were brilliant men but they were just too old when I started. They were finishing up, or a lot of them were after retiring. I was lucky enough to play a year or two with some of them and they were real no-nonsense Waterford men.

I thought they were brilliant men to go through the 70s and 80s. I saw them playing when I was a young fella. They were similar to ourselves; they were good enough to beat everyone but probably not prepared as well as most teams in Munster.

I looked up to all those players… Pat McGrath, John Galvin, Mossie Walsh… great men! John Galvin was a huge help to me. I was a young lad coming into a set-up. John was a back, I was a back… he was very good to me.

He minded me. John is a real genuine fella.

I always tried to get to the ball first. Inter-county forwards, if you let them get the ball, they're in charge. They dictate then. You're probably taking a chance, but you need to win it, you need to have confidence in your ability to control the ball and do whatever you're going to do with it then.

I always tried to get my hands on the ball first. It didn't always work out that way but I tried the best I could.

I loved the physical battle.

The toughest game I had was against Galway in 1988. That game was no-nonsense stuff. Galway didn't want to be beaten and we were trying to come a little bit. We had a huge battle down in Dungarvan that day, a ferocious battle.

I found it a physically tough game. We beat them and they didn't want to be beaten. I remember in the last couple of minutes of the game they got a sideline ball about 30 yards out and the three Galway full-backs ended up in our square!

They needed a goal to win the game. Conor Hayes, Sylvie Linnane and another fella… they were inside in our square for the last couple of minutes of the game.

I always stayed fit.

I was heavy-ish, so I used to train with soccer teams during the winter. And I never missed a training session with my own club Erins Own, even though I was involved with the county. It was probably to my detriment when I look back on it because you wouldn't be as fresh. I always went training even when I was told not to go!

I used to go down with the lads. I was afraid in case they thought I was too good to train with them. I always went with them, *always*.

It was a probably a bit silly in the end. That's the way I did it. I trained all-year round, more or less. It wasn't a chore. I loved every minute of it.

My own father was a great influence on me. He's a Laois man and he moved to Waterford in the 50s. Two super Erins Own men as well… Paddy Coady, who is no longer with us, he was an county player back in the 70s. And another great influence was Billy Kelly. The three of them were very encouraging.

To be totally honest with you, I loved every single minute of it. I would love to be involved in the set-ups at the moment with the way they're being prepared and the professionalism. *From a personal point of view, could I have put more into it?* I don't know.

My actual career, if you can call it that, was a pleasure.

It was a pleasure to be involved with teams at that level, playing against them and playing for Waterford. It is a pleasure to test yourself against the best.

SHANE AHEARNE

Shane Ahearne joined Gerald McCarthy's management team (above) in 1997, and believes Waterford missed a big opportunity of landing the MacCarthy Cup the following year.

66

WE HAD A big win over Clare in the first round and that was a *big thing* for us in Waterford.

I played the five previous years… 1984 to '88, and we were beaten in the first round of the Munster Championship each time. I was playing five years and I had played five championship matches.

That was the old-fashioned system and people say go back to the knockout! Come 1989, we played Clare, Cork (twice) and Tipperary. Four championship matches, and we were hurling up until July which was a big bonus.

We beat Clare fairly well (5-13 to 1-10). That gave us great confidence going in to play Cork. Things worked out for me. I was centre-forward and it just clicked for me that day. I got four points.

I knew myself at that stage that it was going well for me… and bring it on, like! I was willing to play on anyone! Cork made a few switches; Denis Walsh was moved over onto me. It just happened for me. I was the right age, I was 25. I had a bit of experience.

I was on the team since I was 19.

We had a very up and down existence up to that. A lot of promotion and relegation, and all that. In 1988, Tony Mansfield came in and with the help of Phil Fanning and Ollie Wilkinson, they steadied the ship, got a good discipline and was very committed. He got a bunch of fellas thinking right. I had great time for Tony.

He was an old-fashioned type of manager in that he wasn't one for putting the arm around you type of thing… or anything like that! A bit of fire and thunder in the dressing-room and all that. A very genuine man and we all appreciated the sacrifices and the time he put into it. He was a very straight man.

When the drawn game was over, he said, 'We are the better team and we'll be the better team the next day. We won't let it slip.

'If we're good enough to beat them everywhere today, we'll be good enough the next day. Don't be listening to what's going on out there about Cork never losing a replay and all that.' He was very good that way.

In the replay, Pat Murphy had a great day at full-forward. Ger Cunningham got a head injury and Cork blamed that for letting in five goals. Pat Murphy got two goals against Clare and then three goals against Ger Cunningham.

With about a minute to go, I was on Teddy McCarthy; and Teddy said to me, 'Jaysus ye have us beat… well done Shiner, the best of luck in the final!'

I went, 'F*** off, you!'

We were only two points up and he was trying to shake my hand! It was a bit of gamesmanship before the game was over. When it was over, I went ,'We'll shake hands now alright!' We swapped jerseys. I do remember that.

With about two minutes to go, he wanted to shake my hand!!

I was captain in 1989. I was with Mount Sion and Mount Sion had won the 1988 championship. It was a big thing for me, coming from Ferrybank and all that. I liked it and enjoyed it.

Tony Mansfield wasn't the type of fella now to come to you and say, 'What do you think?' He was very old fashioned in his ways! It didn't put much responsibility on me other than interviews and things like that, and I enjoyed that to tell you the truth!

I had gone to America and I grew a bit of a beard. Then, I brought it back to a moustache. I only kept it for about a year. When I see it now, I laugh at myself!

But all of a sudden, we were playing hurling into July.

We were heading for our fourth Munster Championship match… and someone like me for the previous five years playing one match per year. It was a big boost to Waterford hurling. We had beaten nearly every team around, other than Tipperary, in either league or championship. We felt that we weren't far off the big-time. I do remember going around to different summer camps and you could see hurling was getting strong in clubs around the place.

Tipp hit a good day in the final and we had two men sent-off.

I've said this, and I'll say it again, and I'll say it on record… we were naïve with Tipperary. We were getting hit every bit as hard. We said that we were not going to back down from Tipperary.

We were getting hit all over the place.

We lost the media war after that. A lot of our stuff was reactionary. Tipperary hit us every bit as hard as we hit them, but we were doing it more open than they were doing it.

I was delighted to get an All Star nomination at centre-forward. At the time, there weren't many nominations flying around Waterford. The following year I should have got nominated as well. There were only two players nominated for centre-forward. My name was pulled out at the last minute because I got sent-off in a junior football match sometime during the year and they only found out just beforehand.

Just to be nominated was great and I do remember going to the banquet and all that. It was a big boost for me. It would make you feel that maybe you're starting to arrive.

I had been on an All Star tour in 1987; I went as a replacement.

Cork were champions and Kerry were champions. I went on that All Star trip in 1990 as well. That was to Toronto, a one-off match in Toronto, in the SkyDome.

It was shown live on television in Ireland and live on television coast-to-coast in Canada. It was one of the first indoor stadiums; a big, fancy new stadium.

The stands were moveable so it could be an American Football stadium one week or a baseball stadium the following week. We went there in March 1990. To get a second replacement All Star, it doesn't happen too often. You would normally get one and that's it. I went on two All Star trips even though I never got an All Star itself.

There was something like 30,000 people at that match in the SkyDome. Now, I only came on as a sub but it was actually my birthday! My birthday is March 18 and that was the very day that match was played.

My father Peadar was an out-and-out hurling man. His whole life was about hurling and particularly underage hurling. He never did much at adult level or train many adult teams. His whole life was training underage teams in Ferrybank and being up in the primary school and bringing them all out the back and having training sessions out there.

He started up Peadar's Summer Camp in Ferrybank, it's kind of like a Cúl Camp but it's a little bit more fun. He always said to me, 'If anything ever happens me, you have to keep the summer camp going'. He was only doing it two years when he died, so we kept it going.

Now, it's very successful; we have about 300 kids at it every year. It would have been going 29 years last year, only we had to cancel it because of Covid.

Believe it or not, he would have always been a Kilkenny man but when I started playing for Waterford he turned, let's say! He never missed a match. I played a lot of colleges hurling with WIT and even on a Wednesday afternoon, if we were playing somewhere up the country, my father would get to the match somehow or other.

Every match I ever played, my father was at it.

He brought me to my first hurling All-Ireland final when I was eight years of age, in 1972. In on his lap as they used to say. We went to the All-Ireland every year, no matter who was in it. We'd go to Dublin for the weekend. We had relatives in Dublin and we'd go up on a Friday or a Saturday, and wouldn't come back until a Monday.

The All-Ireland was always the first Sunday in September, so I'd miss the first day back in school because that was always the first Monday in September!

I went in as coach with Gerald McCarthy in 1997.

He spent the first year getting a discipline in the team. For the start of the second year, we just felt that we needed to step it up and we needed to be up and running fitness-wise.

We set up a plan whereby every Sunday morning we'd go training in Fenor for an hour first, and then we'd go down to the sand hills in Tramore for the best part of two hours. It was fairly extreme training every Sunday!

It goes back to a man that died only recently by the name of Paddy 'Stinger' Ryan in Waterford.

Paddy was more a judo man and a soccer man.

He was never at a hurling match until myself and a first cousin of mine John 'Doxer' Burns got Stinger over to train Ferrybank. It was physical training and we won the junior hurling in 1995, after a lot of years knocking at the door.

I was back with Ferrybank at this stage. Stinger brought us down to the sand hills in Tramore. It was a revelation to me; it was fantastic training. I always loved training. I just thought this was brilliant.

We did that for something like six weeks with Waterford.

I remember the first morning we did it and when we got back, just going around shaking hands with everyone. You could see the pride in fellas. It was tough but there was a sense of achievement that they had completed it. Every Sunday, I was upping it and upping it and upping it.

By the end of the sixth week of doing it, we were on the Nutron diet as well and the whole atmosphere was fantastic. That was the start of 1998 and that was when Waterford hurling revived itself, if you know what I mean.

We started that programme a day or two after Christmas. So, we had that going on and the Nutron diet going on.

Then, Gerald started introducing gym work.

Before training in Fraher Field, we did gym work in the Park Hotel or the Clonea Strand or the Gold Coast Hotel. We did an hour in the gym, and then over to Fraher Field to the Showgrounds for physical training or what have you. The effort that went in early in 1998 was really phenomenal. It showed by the end of the year.

We lost an All-Ireland semi-final by a point and should have won, and possibly could have won an All-Ireland that year. It's still a big regret.

In 1998, we missed a big chance to break our duck and win that All-Ireland.

99

BRIAN FLANNERY

WATERFORD 0-20 KERRY 1-9
Munster SHC Quarter-Final
Austin Stack Park
MAY 24, 1998

Brian Flannery with Justin McCarthy after Waterford's historic victory in the Munster final in 2002, four years after he made the big decision to transfer from his native Tipperary.

★ **WATERFORD:** B Landers; T Feeney, S Cullinane, **B Flannery**; S Frampton, F Hartley, B Greene; T Browne (0-2), P Queally; D Shanahan (0-6), K McGrath (0-3), D Bennett (0-1); B O'Sullivan, A Kirwan (0-1), P Flynn (0-6). Subs: M White (0-1) for O'Sullivan, S Daly for Bennett.

★ **KERRY:** J Healy; T Cronin, S McIntyre, I Brick; Pat Cronin, M McCarthy, WJ Leen; B O'Sullivan (0-4), R Gentleman (0-2); Padraig Cronin, C Walsh, T Maunsell (0-1); V Dooley, I Maunsell, M Slattery (0-2). Subs: JM Dooley (1-0) for I Maunsell, T O'Connell for V Dooley, M O'Regan for Gentleman.

THE ACTION

WATERFORD WERE PUSHED all the way by Kerry in Tralee just a week after Gerald McCarthy's side lost the National League final to Cork.

The Kingdom shocked the Déise in the 1993 Munster Championship at Walsh Park and memories of that afternoon came flooding back when the outsiders levelled the match with 12 minutes left through Richard Gentleman. It proved to be Kerry's last score, however, as the visitors knocked over eight unanswered points through Dave Bennett, Anthony Kirwan, Dan Shanahan, Paul Flynn, Tony Browne and Micheal White to wrap up a hard-earned win.

Tipperary native Brian Flannery made his championship debut for Waterford at corner-back instead of Mark O'Sullivan. With 4,106 fans in attendance, the away team led by nine points to four at the break. The home side started the better. Points from Michael Slattery, Brendan O'Sullivan and Gentleman left the green and gold 4-2 up after nine minutes. Déise goalkeeper Brendan Landers also stopped O'Sullivan's first-half penalty after a foul on Vincent Dooley.

Man of the Match Dan Shanahan struck four first-half points for the favourites. The Lismore attacker finished the afternoon with six from play. Flynn, Ken McGrath and Tony Browne also split the posts.

Kerry introduced John Mike Dooley and Tom O'Connell for the second period and they made an immediate impact. The two subs combined as Dooley kicked the ball to the net. Gentleman then made it all square on 58 minutes (1-9 to 0-12).

Dave Bennett replied immediately to put Waterford back in front. Shanahan and Flynn added two each with Tony Browne, Anthony Kirwan and Micheal White also on target. Mission accomplished.

★★★★★

66

I'LL ALWAYS HAVE a great sense of gratitude that Waterford gave me my chance to play senior inter-county hurling. That will never desert me.

I came to Waterford in 1991. I played minor with Tipperary in both 1991 and '92; interestingly enough, we lost to Waterford in the '92 Munster final replay! I was in college in Waterford at that stage.

When I finished college then, I started working in Waterford. In 1994, I transferred to Mount Sion. I won an All-Ireland under-21 in 1995 with Tipperary while playing my club hurling in Waterford, which was relatively unusual. I was on the Tipp senior panel then all of 1995 and was on at the start of '96 and let go then during the league. Father Tom Fogarty was the manager at that stage. I was kind of in the wilderness then for a couple of years.

When your club hurling is in Waterford, from a Tipperary point of view, you're out of sight and out of mind.

Coming into 1997, Len Gaynor was after taking over as manager. Shortly after he was appointed, my home club Kiladangan had a celebration night to honour the 1971 Tipperary team that won an All-Ireland intermediate title; a local player Paddy Kelly was captain and my late father was a selector. I was at the function to represent the family and I remember specifically Len gave a speech about the importance of your club and sticking with your club through thick and thin! I kind of felt it was somewhat pointed or maybe I was looking a bit too much into it!

As a player who had just won an All-Ireland under-21, I was keeping an eye on things. I counted that year that Tipp had used 62 players between league, championship, challenge games, tournament games and pitch openings… and I didn't get a shout for any of those! So, I reckoned that the message was quite clear then that the chances of playing senior inter-county with Tipperary were very much gone. I had no conversation with Len Gaynor. None whatsoever. When I looked through the list of players that were being used and I wasn't featuring, it was very much a case of that ship had sailed.

Around the same time, I picked up an injury in 1997, around April. I saw a specialist in Ardkeen and at 23 years of age, I was advised to give up hurling due to a groin injury that I had. That was a pretty big thing at the time.

The actual injury that it turned out to be was Gilmore's groin hernia, which is typically an overuse injury, quite common with soccer professionals at the time. I only found that out after. I remember coming home that day depressed and one of the lads I was sharing a house with said to me, 'Jesus, get a second opinion!'

And he had a contact for Doctor Brian Spillane in Limerick, a former Irish rugby international. When he discussed my case, he immediately recognised that the symptoms were for Gilmore's groin hernia and he referred me on to a surgeon in Dublin, who was Gerry McEntee, the former Meath footballer. Within another week or that, I was in Dublin sitting in a nice, comfortable leather seat in the Mater Private.

Gerry kind of laughed, looking at the referral form from Doctor Spillane which read… '23-year-old, former inter-county hurler'.

'How could you be a former anything at 23?' Gerry asked me.

He told me I wasn't going to do any more damage. I wanted to play the county championship with Mount Sion that summer, so he set the surgery for the autumn once the championship was finished. So, I played championship with Mount Sion that year. The surgery happened then in November of 1997 and, following it, I had a 10-week programme to complete to get back to full fitness.

It's a fitness programme that I did every pre-season after that because it had me in fantastic shape by the time December 1997 came around. I was off work and more or less training full-time for a number of weeks. The 10-week programme… I carried it out to the letter.

Around the same time, I had a chance meeting in Muldoon's nightclub in Waterford one night, where I ran into Shane Ahearne! He was in as selector with Gerald McCarthy; they were just after completing their first year, and he asked me if I would be interested in playing. At that stage, I didn't have anything to lose. It wasn't a question of Tipperary or Waterford; it was a question of do I want to play senior hurling with Waterford or not play senior hurling at all.

I said I'd give it a go. It's an ambition that every player has.

Over the years, I would have played Fitzgibbon Cup hurling with Waterford and I was always playing against the likes of Brian Lohan, Seánie McMahon… and I was looking at them going on playing senior inter-county and I was thinking… *If I can live with them at Fitzgibbon Cup, I'm good enough to play senior inter-county.*

I went in training in December 1997 with Waterford.

I distinctly remember we were doing circuits and weights in St Augustine's in Abbeyside and then we'd go across to Fraher Field to do more running! It was like we were doing two sessions every night! Interestingly, the first guy who came across the dressing-room to shake hands and wish me the best of luck was Mark O'Sullivan from Lismore.

We both probably knew that we were going to be vying for one of two positions in the full-back line. It was nice and a great mark of the player that Mark O'Sullivan was. That was the first night and after a while then, you're part of it and you just get on with it. One of the advantages I had, coming off the groin operation and the 10-week recovery programme, was that I was quite fit at the time. I was in good shape.

The league had been a bit up and down. As a team, we went well. I dropped out of the team by the time we got to the league semi-final. We beat Limerick and the league final then against Cork, I was a sub that day but I still remember running onto the field and the roar of the crowd.

It was a huge occasion and the bandwagon was up and running in Waterford at that stage to be back in a league final. A huge crowd inside in Thurles. Even as a substitute, pucking around before the game, there was that sense of occasion. Something was happening in Waterford hurling.

We only lost by a few points. I was driving at the time and Derek McGrath travelled with me. Neither of us played in the final and we were going home that evening and we were passing through Danesfort and we noticed there was a match going on. As young fellas would, we pulled in. Kilkenny were playing Tipperary in a challenge game. We just went onto the bank and watched it, the last few minutes.

'Maybe we can beat these sort of lads.'

The first game up was Kerry in the first round of the Munster Championship in Tralee. It was a bit of surprise to be selected. The Tuesday before the game, I was just lazily pucking around and Paul Kelly, who was a hurley carrier at the time, was shouting over at me that I'd want to be a bit sharper next Sunday against Kerry.

I was kind of looking at him as if he had two heads. *What's he talking about it?* It wouldn't have been on the cards. Sure enough, when the team was announced, I got the nod. I remember the local papers... Phil Fanning in the *News & Star* more or less said that it was an error by the management team to change the back line from the league final.

I was thinking... *Thanks Phil.*

It was on in Tralee; it wasn't Tipperary, it wasn't Cork. It was kind of low-key; it wasn't on TV or anything. Because of the distance in travelling, there wasn't a huge Waterford crowd at the game either.

We're talking about 1998, only five years after Kerry had beaten Waterford in the Munster Championship in Walsh Park. It was a game I was actually at because I was in college in Waterford at the time. I was on the bank and I just couldn't believe what I was watching. That was a huge shock, and this was only five years later.

The sense was that because Waterford had got to the league final that this was very much expected to be an easy victory.

In the first couple of minutes, a high ball came into the square and I held out my marker, as you do, to let ball go directly into Brendan Landers in goal... and the referee was running from the middle of the field with his arms stretched out indicating a penalty! I was thinking... *This could be a nightmare.*

We recovered and I played well after that. It's a game that's forgotten, apart from the small attendance and the players involved. As we were going down the stretch, Kerry had brought the game level and Brendan Landers brought off a great save. Had we conceded that, we would have gone a goal down.

For the last 15 or 20 minutes, I switched out from corner-back to wing back. Dan Shanahan came into it and having gone from level, with 10 minutes to go, we hit eight points without reply. If somebody was looking at the score on the nine o'clock news that night it looked like, as expected, a comfortable victory for Waterford, but it was anything else.

There was a sense of panic at one stage on the sideline. They were actually over close to me and they shouted at me to go from corner out to wing, maybe because I was just in front of them! It was a little bit hairy. It was one of those occasions that you won't read too much about or hear too much about, it was a low profile game, but it could have been a disaster for that team.

It could have gone totally wrong but, thankfully, it didn't. We survived, I survived and we gained that bit of confidence.

The next day against Tipperary was the big win. Obviously, for me personally to beat Tipperary was a big deal. It was a heightened sense of pressure, a heightened sense of wanting to do well.

Doctor Tom Higgins gave me a couple of tablets, a couple of paracetamol. I had flu symptoms that morning so I didn't do much of a warm-up beforehand. I remember going into the stand in Páirc Uí Chaoimh to watch some of the minor match. There were two guys behind me, John Costigan, who became a trustee of the GAA, and Tom Moloughney, who had won All-Irelands with Tipperary back in the 60s.

John was Tipperary minor manager during my time and both of them wished me well. Tom shook my hand and he mentioned, 'I knew your father!' which was very poignant for me. This was the big-time, this was where you were rubbing shoulders with the big players. *Could I survive in that company?*

In the *Nenagh Guardian*, after we had beaten Tipperary, in one of the commentary pieces it was said… *The best player for Tipperary on the day was wearing Waterford colours.*

They talk about the 90s being the hurling revolution years and Waterford announced themselves in 1998, there's no doubt about that. Unfortunately, we didn't finish the job. We lost to Kilkenny by a point in the All-Ireland semi-final. In retrospect, 1998 was as good an opportunity to bridge the gap to '59 as there has been given the circumstances. We held that Kilkenny forward line with DJ Carey, but we didn't get enough scores on the day. That was an opportunity lost.

It's hard to underplay the importance of Gerald McCarthy to that team. He really broke down the inter-club rivalry. I remember instances, even before I hurled with Waterford, where it was nearly more important for guys to hurl with their clubs than with the county. We were playing a club challenge match and lads, instead of going training in Walsh Park, played a club *challenge* game.

That connection to the county team, until Gerald came, wasn't as strong as it should have been. That struck me, as an outsider initially in Waterford. If you were a club in Tipperary and you had a player on the county team, you were delighted and honoured. There would be no question of players not going to train with their county... *to go play a match with their club.*

You didn't have that same sense in Waterford. Maybe it was because of the lack of success. Maybe players didn't see the potential there to win honours... 1998 changed all that.

I always had a great sense of loyalty and gratitude for the fact that Waterford had given me my chance to play senior inter-county. There was an occasion, at the start of 2001, that Gerald McCarthy drove to Waterford to specifically make sure that I was on board that year. There was a strong rumour, which had a bit of merit in it, that Tipperary wanted me to go back. I would have discussed the option of returning with Nicky English, who was Tipperary manager at the time.

You see, 2000, the year before, would have been one of my best years. I picked up one of those WLR monthly awards in 2000. We lost to Tipperary by three points and on the strength of it, I won a bit of crystal. At that stage, I would have been seen as a safe pair of hands and, rightly or wrongly, I don't know whether it's a compliment or an insult, I was seen as a man who played well on the big days.

Some of my best games were probably against Tipperary back then.

My own feelings on it were that Waterford had given me my opportunity and I felt a sense of loyalty to Waterford and to the players I had trained with and played with. I had captained Waterford in 1999 as well. I made the decision that I was staying put, that my life was in Waterford.

I actually felt that it would have been the wrong thing to do. I would have felt uncomfortable. I remember even discussing it at the time with some of the lads at the club. I was happy with the decision I made; I was making the decision for the right reasons. Later on that year, 2001, Tipperary won an All-Ireland. I was in the Sweep Bar, watching the final with clubmates and I can honestly say that I never had as much as a second thought about whether I had made the right decision or not.

2002 was a huge highlight.

I have a picture at home somewhere with the Munster cup. Brazil won the World Cup the same day so Ronaldo had the World Cup and I had the Munster cup! It was in the *Independent*. Waterford have won three Munster titles since but to bridge that 39-year gap... the importance of it at the time was huge.

We now had a generation of players who feared nobody and went out every day expecting to win. I don't think that was always the case.

The overriding thing would be a sense of gratitude. It was a bit of a leap of faith for Gerald McCarthy and Shane Ahearne, as much as it was for me. Thankfully, it worked out. *No regrets.*

99

SEÁN CULLINANE
(& STEPHEN FRAMPTON)

WATERFORD 0-21 TIPPERARY 2-12
Munster SHC Semi-Final
Páirc Uí Chaoimh
JUNE 7, 1998

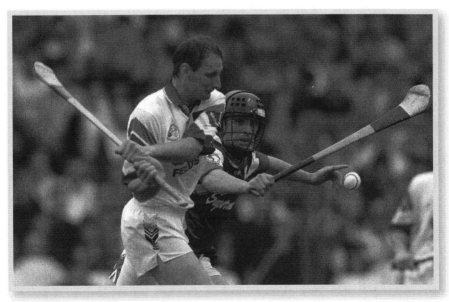

Seán Cullinane clears the ball against Galway's Alan Kerins in the All-Ireland quarter-final in 1998, but it was the Munster semi-final that year when Waterford finally defeated Tipperary that gave him his proudest day in blue and white.

★ **WATERFORD:** B Landers; B Flannery, **S Cullinane**, T Feeney; **S Frampton**, F Hartley, B Greene; T Browne (0-2), P Queally; D Shanahan (0-2), K McGrath (0-4), D Bennett; B O'Sullivan (0-2), A Kirwan (0-1), P Flynn (0-10).

★ **TIPPERARY:** B Cummins; P Shelley, M Ryan, L Sheedy; B Horgan, A Butler, Conal Bonnar; Colm Bonnar, T Dunne (0-2); L Cahill (0-3), L McGrath (0-1), J Leahy (0-1); D Ryan (0-1), E O'Neill (1-3), M Kennedy (0-1). Subs: B O'Meara (1-0) for Colm Bonnar, C Gleeson for Conal Bonnar, P Kelly for McGrath.

THE ACTION

A FAMOUS WIN by the Lee for the Déise, as the 1998 league finalists sent the 1997 All-Ireland finalists packing. A long hot summer was in store.

Waterford wizard Paul Flynn was Man of the Match with 10 points (five frees and five from play) as he tormented the Tipp defence. Ken McGrath got four while Dan Shanahan, Billy O'Sullivan and Tony Browne chipped in with two each.

Captain Stephen Frampton led from the front as the Ballygunner No 5 stamped his authority against Tipp talisman John Leahy. Seán Cullinane was another towering figure at full-back.

A Eugene O'Neill goal gave Tipp a 1-10 to 0-8 half-time lead. Waterford overtook their opponents on the restart with seven unanswered points in a dazzling 13-minute spell. Flynn and O'Sullivan were on fire in the full-forward line. A goal from Tipp sub Brian O'Meara levelled the match with nine minutes left. Waterford bounced back from that body-blow with another Flynn point.

As time ticked down, Waterford keeper Brendan Landers made a double save from Michael Kennedy and Liam Cahill. A goal would have brought Tipp level. The young shot-stopper answered his critics. 'I have had to listen to a lot of negative talk about my goalkeeping this year but I have stuck with it, thanks to the support and encouragement of my dad Donal, who helped me through difficult times.'

Entering injury-time, Declan Ryan hit a ground stroke just wide of the post. Tommy Dunne tapped over a late free instead of going for the jugular. In the third minute of injury-time, Shanahan fetched the puck-out from Lismore clubmate Landers, pointed and punched the air in pure delight.

★ ★ ★ ★ ★

66

FOR ME, 1998 stands out a mile. It was my best year. I spent 14 years playing and training for that.

It was our first year going out taking on the big guns and beating them. We were competing with The Big Three. After being there for 10 years and getting a lot of bad beatings off these lads, to be going out week-in, week-out and competing with them was unbelievable. The team struggled for years to get up to that level and to finally be there was an amazing feeling. After 10 years of trying to beat Tipperary in the championship, we eventually did it in 1998. That was the one that stood out more than anything.

That year was a major turnaround for me, and for the team in general.

Gerald McCarthy came along and things changed. Taking on Cork and Tipp was always a struggle in the early 90s. You'd be hoping that they'd have a bad day and you'd have a good day to have any chance of staying in the game even. When Gerald came along in 1997, that changed. We were going out with a self-belief that we could beat these lads and to actually do it then was a tremendous feeling.

I had a quiet day myself in 1998 against Tipp.

I didn't have many balls to deal with. They got two *soft* goals, I know that. I'm after seeing them a couple times since and they were *two soft goals*. Eugene O'Neill in the first-half... a breaking ball and he pulled on it. And then, one of the subs Brian O'Meara pulled one-handed in the second-half.

They got two lucky breaks and they stuck them.

The emotion after beating them was the thing that stood out. Everything knitted together. There was a self-belief that day that we could do it and when we finally did, it was a great feeling to have.

A couple of things stood out for me during my career and they all happened in 1998. The National League semi-final... when we ran out. I'll never forget the roar of the crowd that day, it was just unbelievable. You often hear the saying the hair stood on the back of your neck, well it certainly did that day for me. It was just unreal.

The second one was when the final whistle went against Tipp.

That feeling of emotion and winning. I remember being out on the field for ages and ages after it. After a win like that, everyone just wants to soak it up.

Everyone was on a high. My father and my uncle John Joe never missed any game… and my mother when she was alive. She died earlier that year. She died that January.

For my father and my uncle John Joe, it was extra special for them.

The Nutron diet was hard but it really worked for me. I probably lost too much weight but I felt unbelievably fit. I had loads of energy even though I didn't look it! I looked like a skeleton really at the time! Energy-wise and fitness-wise, I felt absolutely terrific and it worked really well.

I remember my wife trying to make this brown bread and it was more like cardboard! She thought she wasn't making it right so she gave the ingredients that I got to several other people, including Una Keating from Passage. Now, Una Keating would be a connoisseur of brown bread and it still turned out the same!

It was tough. You needed to really stick to it. Food-wise, you just couldn't eat anything out of a tin or a packet, nothing with preservatives in it. I hadn't a reaction to it. One or two players struggled a lot with it. I didn't have any great problems with any of the food, just the lack of it!

I pulled my hamstring in the drawn Munster final against Clare. I was lucky enough; I was nearly 30 before I pulled a hamstring. I used to be always laughing at people, asking, 'Is a hamstring something you fry up in a pan!' Suddenly, I was playing Ballygunner one day and I pulled one and I struggled with them then for a couple of years.

I'd always be back within 10 days.

Whatever damage I used to do, it was always 10 days. We only had seven days until the replay against Clare. We tried everything. A friend of mine, who used to play football with Gaultier, Pat Lee was after setting up a clinic with the dry needle and I went down to him every day, sometimes twice a day, trying to get it right.

I was down with him twice a day for four or five days trying to get this repaired in time for the weekend. I did a fitness test in Urlingford on the way up and it just wasn't right. When you're playing at that level… not a hope. The replay didn't go our way but I was right then for the Galway game.

I was happy enough; I settled for that.

If I was carrying a bit of an injury, I wasn't great at letting them know. I'd just keep going. I'd work on it myself. There's a hill across the road from us and I spent a lot of time running up and down it backwards! Especially with the hamstring.

Shay Fitzpatrick had this regime for me with hill work: if you can't sprint forward, go up it backwards. I spent a lot of time out there. I did a good bit of work on it. Whatever way the hamstring is, you could go backwards up the hill no bother. It's a steep enough hill, you wouldn't be moving that far!

In the close season, over Christmas, I'd do a lot of work. I'd never not do anything. A couple of nights a week or whatever just to keep myself in some sort of nick. When I got married, I moved up the road, a half a mile.

There's a more level field here. In the close season, November or December, I spent a lot of time out there keeping myself in nick. Little things like that. I don't know was everybody at it... maybe they were. I know they are now.

You're training and you have everything planned out in front of you. It was a little different back with us. The training went from an hour, an hour and a bit in 1988 two nights a week, to an hour five or six times a week with Gerald McCarthy... and some of the sessions were maybe three hours.

The hours that went into training in my time really changed from the early years to the latter years. It seems to go a step further every year.

When you're playing in the full-back line, you meet a lot of tough opponents. Nicky English caused me enough problems in my early years. Joe Deane caused me more problems than anyone, very elusive. He used to catch the hurley wrong and I didn't know which way he was going. He was like Paul Flynn, if he got the ball out in front of you, you didn't know if he was going left or right. That's a major problem!

With the way he caught the hurley, you could never hook him; you could never get near him. He caused me a lot of problems over the years. If you go out every day and you're marking Nicky English or Pat Fox or John Fitzgibbon or DJ Carey... *you're going to have some problems!* You go out and you do the best you can.

I wasn't blessed with pace but I had a good reading of the game and I didn't panic. A lot of times, I could get a hook or a block or a flick in. Whatever you could. That's about all you can do. It comes down to the belief in your own ability. I tried to play the game that suited myself as best I could.

I really tried hard. Even when we were doing the hard training in 1998, I used to end up doing bits on my own as well, extra bits, to make sure that I was better than the fella I was on, if I could at all.

I liked to play from the front, so you've got to trust your own ability. It's not an easy place to play in the full-back line. Full-back is even harder than the corners. If you make a mistake at full-back, nine times out of 10 it will end up in the net, I'll put it that way to you.

You can't go out thinking about that, you go out there fully confident that you're there to do a job and you do it the best you can.

The emotions were mixed, very *mixed* when Waterford won the Munster title in 2002. Of course, I was absolutely thrilled that we won it, but gutted after 14 years to only miss it by a couple of weeks. I went into the dressing-room after the game and one thing led to another… and I went back on the bus.

We stopped at Youghal bridge and walked across it… and I was as proud as any Waterford man.

STEPHEN FRAMPTON

Stephen Frampton leads the Waterford team in the parade before the Munster final against reigning All-Ireland champions Clare in 1998 in Semple Stadium.

"

I HAD ALL sorts of issues in the build-up to that Tipp game to be quite honest!

My wife Anne-Marie was in hospital since the Friday night. She gave birth to our daughter Emma, so it was a really long day in the hospital. She had gone early so we weren't expecting it.

Prior to that, I had a little bit of an issue with a calf injury. I was frightened of my life that it was going to come against me in the match. The heel was nearly coming out of my boot, I had such a big heel wedge to try and protect the calf! So, I was up all night during my wife's labour and, on top of that, I was just worried and so apprehensive about breaking down in middle of the match with the calf.

I was thrilled to get through it to be honest. It was probably adrenaline that got me through it. I was also very apprehensive about marking John Leahy.

It never happened me before where I was given a specific job on the day of a match. It was the first time that happened at inter-county level. I was to mark him wherever he went. John Leahy was a fantastic hurler at that stage; he was one of the top forwards in the country and had a reputation.

Gerald McCarthy said, 'Look, if we can keep him under wraps, we'll go a long way towards beating Tipperary!' They had a lot of other great players but Leahy was the type of player that the Tipperary supporters loved – the type of high profile player he was… that if he was going well, he could inspire the rest of the team and inspire the whole crowd.

There was a little bit of added pressure with that but I was happy to do it. I was very apprehensive about it, but very determined… *I'm going to play my part.*

We had a bit of a battle that day.

That was all part and parcel of it. I was gutted with Pete Finnerty's commentary; he was on *The Sunday Game* that night. I thought he was a little bit negative towards me, which I thought was kind of ironic because he was a combative and aggressive half-back himself. I was a little bit disappointed the way he worded the battle that we had between us.

It was almost as if I bullied Leahy. I didn't bully him really, the two of us had a good go and that was it. There was no such thing as bullying, it was good and tough, and that was it.

I thought I hurled quite well that day but all the talk was about hitting John Leahy. My hurling performance on the day was overshadowed by the whole 'John Leahy thing'.

After the match, the buzz in Páirc Uí Chaoimh was fantastic. It was palpable, the excitement from Waterford people. We had got to a National League final so we had done well… and that was our first national final in an awful long time. It was all building from there really and then to win a match against one of the big guys in the championship was dreamland.

I have to mention Tom Coffey and Tom McCarthy. I think I might have made a comment down in the Imperial Hotel on South Mall, inside in the reception, that I must get home to see my good wife. They said, 'Sure we'll give you a lift home'.

The bus wasn't going to be leaving for a few hours. They brought me down the road, down to the hospital and they went back to Dungarvan so they had a double journey to do. They were so good.

That was the buzz that was about that day, and the goodwill. They brought me down to the hospital to Anne-Marie and my daughter Emma. It was a great day. A lot of people still talk about that now when they meet me! It's funny what people remember.

I was captain that year, and it was a breakthrough year. It was our first Munster Championship win in quite a while and it was a catalyst for us. We ended up beating Galway in an All-Ireland quarter final as a result of it. We got to an All-Ireland semi-final… and lack of experience beat us in that game. We only lost by a point.

It was a *nearly* year.

Gerald brought a new professionalism to training… to match preparation and to team preparation. Stuff that other counties would have taken for granted. We started to get a little bit more gear, a few pairs of boots and that. That was all very new to us.

He was coming from a county like Cork where all that stuff was quite standard. It was fantastic to be appreciated and see that we were starting to be backed by the County Board and that there was investment in the team. Gerald brought that with him and he also brought a steeliness to the training. He trained us really, *really* hard.

We did an awful lot of work down in the sand dunes in Tramore. Running up that Baldy Man, I'll never forget it! Absolute, pure torture!

Our trainer Shane Ahearne took great satisfaction in that side of it! It was horrible training but he really got us in great shape. He was trying to hit on every sort of angle of preparation. We also went on the Nutron diet, which was all the fad at the time. Not only were we being prepared on the pitch, but all of a sudden nutrition was coming into it which was completely alien to us. All very new and all very professional.

All I remember is… *I was eating broccoli until I turned green!*

Broccoli and salmon, I remember that! They're the two things that I remember… and vegetable stir fries. It did the trick. A lot of fellas trimmed up, including myself. That's what Gerald brought to it. He brought us to a new level of preparation and a new level of training.

I was around a while at that stage; I was on the panel since 1988 so it was my tenth year. There wouldn't have been a whole lot of chat about hurling, only from the real diehard hurling people in those years. There wouldn't have been a whole lot to talk about, to be quite honest!

After that year, it became very popular and it was fashionable around the county and people wanted to talk to you about hurling… people who really only had a passing interest, but all of a sudden, it was popular. You just had to chat away to them but it was great that people wanted to talk about hurling. For years, they didn't have any interest in it.

That was all very good and very positive.

I wouldn't have any regrets about leaving the panel in 2002 under Justin McCarthy. I think I did the right thing; I probably should have done it earlier. But I was very disappointed with the way it was handled, to be quite honest. When I say it was handled, it wasn't *handled*. I was, obviously, from the management point of view, gone past my sell-by date, which is fine, I understand that; I've managed and trained and I'm still involved with teams and have been for a long number of years.

I understand the dynamics of picking teams, and not picking players. It was the way it wasn't dealt with basically. I was not communicated with at all to an extent that, in the end, I just thought… *Look, I need to get out of here!*

From that point of view, it was very disappointing.

I was trying to talk to people that year and nobody would really talk to me, so I didn't have much of a choice really. It was very disappointing. I don't think I would have been all that happy to be part of it in that situation under those circumstances.

Jim and Charlie Ware are my grand-uncles, that's my connection to royalty in hurling! The Wares would have been synonymous with Erins Own in Waterford city and they won multiple county championships. They are a family steeped in GAA history.

Jim Ware was the goalkeeper and captain on the 1948 team. He still is the oldest captain of an All-Ireland winning team. I was always very aware of that.

My granny would have lived with us for a long time. She had a great interest in hurling. It was a great source of inspiration to know that that was part of our background. You'd love to be coming back to the house and talking to her about the matches and showing her medals.

Everybody that I was with had a fantastic influence on my career. Adult players don't realise the influence that individuals have until they grow old and grey like me! There were a lot of really good people in Ballygunner, who accommodated us to play hurling… Willie Hartley, Fergal's father… John Lyons, Calum Lyons' grandfather… and Thomas O'Sullivan were great influences in the early days.

Jim Hennessy in school in Ballygunner, who is a mad Mount Sion man, in the early times with Mr McGinn in National School, they were great men as well. Mick Gaffney at adult level and Pat Flynn… Paul Flynn's father, was a fantastic hurling man.

At inter county-level, Tony Mansfield and Gerald McCarthy.

So many good people.

PETER QUEALLY
(& PAUL FLYNN)

WATERFORD 1-16 CORK 1-15
Munster SHC Semi-Final
Semple Stadium
MAY 26, 2002

Peter Queally breaks away with the ball despite the attention of Timmy McCarthy and John Browne in the Munster semi-final victory over Cork in Semple Stadium in 2002.

★ **WATERFORD:** S Brenner; J Murray, T Feeney, B Flannery; **P Queally**, F Hartley, E Murphy; T Browne (1-0), D Bennett; E Kelly, A Moloney, **P Flynn (0-12)**; J Mullane (0-1), S Prendergast (0-1), E McGrath. Subs: K McGrath (0-2) for Moloney, D Shanahan for Bennett, M White for Mullane, B Greene for E McGrath.

★ **CORK:** D Óg Cusack; W. Sherlock, D O'Sullivan, F Ryan; D Barrett, J Browne, S Óg Ó hAilpín; A Cummins, T McCarthy (0-2); J O'Connor, F McCormack, N McCarthy; B O'Connor (0-8), E Collins (1-1), J Deane (0-3). Subs: P Ryan for McCormack, S McGrath (0-1) for J O'Connor.

THE ACTION

AN INJURY-TIME point from super-sub Ken McGrath secured Waterford's first championship win over Cork since 1989.

McGrath suffered a serious shoulder injury in a challenge game against Dublin a couple of weeks before that but came off the bench after 25 minutes and hit two second-half points. Another sub Brian Greene set up that late, *late* winner. Justin McCarthy had masterminded an unexpected win against his native county.

At a wet and windy Thurles, dead-ball ace Paul Flynn was Man of the Match with a dozen points. This included two frees from more than 100 metres out and three from play.

A goal from Eamonn Collins gave Cork a 1-7 to 0-9 lead at half-time. On 43 minutes, Tony Browne's delivery from midfield skidded off the greasy surface and flew past Donal Óg Cusack into the Cork net. Waterford moved five in front with two points from Flynn and one from McGrath. But the Rebels responded with five unanswered points to bring the sides level by the 66th minute.

In the first minute of injury-time, Peter Queally swept the ball up to Greene. The sub found his Mount Sion clubmate with a hand pass, and McGrath did the rest.

Waterford made front page news the following day after Flynn and Brian Flannery refused to take a drugs test. They were randomly selected, along with Cork's Fergal Ryan and Ben O'Connor, to provide urine samples to National Sports Council tester Al Guy. The Déise pair felt that they hadn't received adequate information about what was involved. They were faced with a 48-week suspension for refusing to comply. After a stand-off at Semple Stadium, both players eventually agreed to give samples at the team hotel.

★★★★★

66

I WOULD HAVE grown up watching Cork giving Waterford hidings, on big championship days... the two Munster finals in the 80s. There was a reverence when it came to the red Cork jersey. To actually go out and beat them in the championship, it added to the whole thing.

For pure euphoria, it's hard to beat the one-point wins.

Especially the way it happened. We got Tony's goal halfway through the second-half which was quite fortuitous... on the greasy surface it squirmed past Donal Óg Cusack. It gave us a buffer which Cork eked back point-by-point-by point. To bring it back level, turn that momentum, get the winner and hold on to get the victory... it was pretty special and it was pretty euphoric at the final whistle.

I was at both the 1982 and '83 Munster finals.

As a family, we went in 1982. All of us. It was a big occasion back then, a big family thing. A huge crowd at it; it must have been nearly a full house. I was only 12 that year. It was such a hiding, the crowd dwindled the following year but I remember myself and my father went. I'd say psychologically back then, it must have been hard for those players to come back the following year, especially against such a good Cork team.

It was very deflating; it was very disappointing. When you witness it at that age, you think to yourself... *Wow, we're miles away from this, we'll never win anything.* You don't think of the bigger picture, things going in cycles.

You're thinking... *We're so far behind Cork!*

As you get older and wiser, you realise that it's not always going to be that way. It was brilliant as a teenage fan to see in the late-80s the draw and the semi-final win in 1989. That was a great thing to be a spectator at.

I was based in Youghal Garda Station at the time. It wasn't as if I was in the middle of them; I was on the periphery of them!

With Youghal, you have a fair auld sprinkling of Waterford people living and working there. It added to the rivalry because of the border town. A lot of that would have been kept from me. I was little bit sheltered from that then; I was only in Youghal about three years at that stage.

There was a lot of interest in it. I remember doing a lot of interviews around it with where I was based; I was probably one of the older members on the panel as well. There would have been a few journalists quizzing me about it and talking about the rivalry and talking it up a bit. So, I was well aware of it!

I preferred not to hold the hurley after training on the Friday night.

It's appetite, it's hunger… I never liked to do anything the day before a game… be it training, a puck-around… anything. I learned that from experience.

You try every kind of approach in your earlier years and see what works. That was the approach that worked for me… leave it there, put it down after the puck-around on the Friday night and don't pick up the hurley again until Sunday.

It's amazing when you go into coaching, you try to preach this philosophy but you can't force it, it's whatever suits people. The approach that worked for me was just leaving it there and not picking it up.

I got a little bit of a buzz or a vibe off it, when I picked it up on Sunday, on match-day.

I missed it and I was looking forward to using it again.

One of the years we got Irish champion boxer Neil Gough in to talk to us and he spoke about triggers. For him, a trigger on a big match-day was a cold shower. Once he had that cold shower, it was his mind telling him… *Right, game on here, it's time to get serious now.*

I used to listen to this tape by Tony Quinn. He was a guru back then. Now there was a lot of mumbo-jumbo in it, but I think it had the same effect as regards… *there's a big game coming up now*… you're listening to this and it's going through your mind.

What it did for me, I don't know, but going back to Neil's thing, it was just a trigger to tell me… *Ok, there's a big game coming up here, time to get serious about it.*

If you're to equate it to anything now, it was a bit of mindfulness. It's something that you wouldn't be going around announcing in a dressing-room! I would have got the absolute piss taken out of me. I kept it very much to myself; I didn't tell anyone about it.

I'd say it was 1999 I started using it. I listened to it in the car. Very much on my own and away from people.

I was marking Niall McCarthy that day.

It was his first game for Cork. Justin McCarthy being our manager, he had the inside track on a lot of the Cork team so he spent the last training session going through each player. When it came to me, he said, 'You're marking this young fella from Carrigtwohill now... Niall McCarthy, he's a bit soft like, you know'.

I was like, 'Okay, okay!'

I knew nothing about him, I took Justin's word for it. As we all know at this stage, Niall McCarthy is far from soft!

Before the ball was thrown in, I said I'd test his ribs and gave him a dunt. If I did, he gave it back twice as hard! I whispered to myself... *Ah Jesus. You got that one wrong Justin, I tell you that much!*

I wasn't thanking Justin for it anyway! We had a good tussle in fairness! He is very strong, a very good hurler. He didn't score that day but he did go on to achieve great things in a Cork jersey. He was an integral part of their double-All-Ireland-winning team. That's what I remember about the contest, the initial welcome to championship hurling that was given back in spades!

Wing back was my favourite position. It was a little bit easier to face the ball and position myself. Sometimes in midfield, the game can pass you by.

I wouldn't have been known for scoring either... so slipping back another line, I didn't feel under pressure to chip in with a point or two. Aerial ability as well... I was comfortable enough in the air with a high ball coming down. That would have been my strongest attribute, I think.

Towards the end of the game, when it was level, I had a bit of an involvement in the last score. Tom Feeney... a low ball came into his corner, I think he might have been on Joe Deane. He beat him out to it, showed brilliant control and as he approached, I became available and he passed it out to me.

I remember hitting a low ball into the forwards that was nearly intercepted but, thankfully, it wasn't and it came to Brian Greene who off-loaded it to Ken McGrath. Ken had just come on; he shouldn't have even come on, he didn't start that day because of a bad shoulder injury... and he got the winning score.

In the immediate aftermath, when the final whistle went, I just remember pure euphoria. I was beside Tony Browne and it wasn't a case of fist-pumping... it was jumping and screaming and crying. I remember his brother Tommy coming in as well; he must have beaten the stewards! He was there so we had a bit of an embrace. Screaming and shouting and jumping up and down. Just the euphoria of it is something that stands out, even to this day.

We had a few drinks but it wasn't the usual haunt. We had the grub in the Anner Hotel where we normally did. It was a pub on the way down to the Anner… we never went there before. With the traffic back then, it was nearly easier to walk back to the Anner from Semple Stadium. We were looking into pubs as we went along to spot a quiet one but it was nearly impossible.

Up near the Anner, it was starting to quieten down a bit so we did spot a quietish pub and went upstairs there and had a few drinks to ourselves. We got five tables up on the second floor and 20 of us sat around having a bit of a chat and that was nice. Nice to get the moments to yourself without the supporters coming up.

I remember talking to Tony. I don't know how it stands out, but I remember him saying that this is special for us… us fellas that have been there a long time more so than the younger fellas. He was right, it was. Sometimes, I won't say you take it for granted, but it means that little more when you're there for 10 or 12 years.

After the Munster final, we called into the Garda Station in Youghal. After the drinks we had in the hotel and the drinks we had on the bus, a pitstop was called for. I don't know why the Garda Station, maybe just the fact that I was stationed there, the lads decided to use it. We filtered in and every nook and cranny was used.

Funny enough a few guards that I worked with were there and sure they were delighted. They saw the cup and that.

'Let's get a picture!'

Sure enough, the station camera that we used for pictures, the battery was gone. It would have been a nice photo to have. We still have the memories.

I had the memories of being a spectator and the three big losses. I remember going, by default, to the 1990 replay. It was a brilliant match… Cork and Tipp. The boss man in Dawn Meats was Peter Queally. I was working at Dawn Meats. I had a game on Saturday and I came back to Carroll's Cross and Louis Dunne, the proprietor, says, 'I've an envelope here for you, Seamus Grant dropped it in.'

And it was two Munster final tickets!

Myself and my girlfriend at the time headed off early the following morning up to Thurles to watch the match. As it turned out, they weren't meant for me at all! They were for the boss man. I wouldn't say he was too impressed with it!

I got to sit up in probably the best seats in Semple Stadium and watch it. I remember the likes of Conal Bonnar warming up in front of me and thinking... *Wow, how good a hurler is he...* and you're envious and you're dreaming of what it would be like to even just play in one, let alone go on and win one.

It was nice 12 years later to fulfil that dream.

I would be happy with my lot. I got the most out of it. I knew my limitations; I knew I wasn't the most skilful or the most stylish hurler. I knew I was from a small junior club in Ballydurn so everything I got, I earned. It was a work ethic and a workrate that got me there.

It was something I always had as a young person and as a hurler, that work ethic... farming background, a grafter.

I have no regrets, I got to play with brilliant hurlers.

I was very lucky to represent Munster in the Railway Cup. In those three years, when I was with Munster, I lined out at midfield and I was with John Leahy the first year, whom I had great battles with and great time for... Tommy Dunne the second year, a supreme artist of a hurler, and the third year was the cream of them all... one of my favourite all-time hurlers... Ciaran Carey.

They're great memories and something that I'm very proud of.

PAUL FLYNN

Paul Flynn always chose to practice his frees in solitude, in Ballygunner, far away from the Waterford camp (above, he shoots against Cork in the historic victory in the Munster Championship in Semple Stadium in 2002.

"

I RANG JUSTIN McCarthy and I said I wouldn't be around for the championship.

He said not to do anything hasty! Seán Cullinane and Stephen Frampton did the hasty thing, I suppose, and said they had enough of this. I was 27, but I thought I had enough hurling done too.

Any time we needed to win, we just seemed to lose. I was disillusioned.

He said, 'Go off to America and come back!'

I came back the week after. They were training in Dunhill one night and I went out. It was the time of year, late-April, the evenings were longer… every player likes the late-spring or early summer for training; the ground getting a bit harder, the balls drier, the summer game starting to evolve. John Mullane had come on the scene, Eoin Kelly had come on the scene; we had more options up front.

The defeat to Limerick in 2001 was particularly hard, the one down in Cork when we were 11 points up. That was a hard one to take. We started questioning ourselves.

Is it worthwhile actually continuing on?

The win came from an unexpected place. I remember one night up in Mount Sion, we were training and we asked Colm Bonnar, who was in charge of the physical side of it, could we do more running?

Colm obviously had the plan. We did our hurling, we did our few sprints and that was it.

It was Justin's first year. We had a very bad league. We weren't doing any physical training; it was all hurling training. May 26 was the day.

Ken McGrath was injured, Brian Greene was injured… Cork had a strike that year, it was a crossroads in the GAA. We were total underdogs.

I remember we played Kilkenny in a challenge match about two or three weeks before it. We were in disarray. But it just clicked on the day.

Cork were in disarray too with the strike and the bad publicity and so on.

The match went well for me personally. Some days you're in the right place, some days you can't get into the right place. Cork play hurling. We knew it was going to be a *hurling match*; it wasn't going to be a hacking session or anything like that.

It went well for a lot of us. We don't beat Cork that often. It was 13 years since we beat them. In 2004, when we beat them in the Munster final, that bridged a 45-year gap.

I remember the first-half in particular; we had a bit of a breeze with us, and it turned out to be a wet afternoon. We decided that day that we would let Cork throw in all the sliotars. Donal Óg Cusack used to have a bag of balls in the net and he used to think he was pulling a quick one by switching them to All Star balls.

We decided that we would let them throw in as many as they wanted because the rim on the All Star ball was smaller at the time than the O'Neill's ball, so we probably preferred playing with that.

That Sunday night we had a right few pints in Thurles. It was a massive turning point.

In terms of practicing frees, I would throw eight balls across the pitch from sideline to sideline and I'd allow myself seven out of eight. If I missed more than two, I'd start again.

I'd rather do it on my own.

I never practiced frees really before training or at training. I'd always do it on my own up in Ballygunner. It was therapy too. *Time on your own.* Practice. Some days it could take 20 minutes, other days it could take two hours!

It was just repetition. The most important thing about taking frees is having the ball in a consistent place when you lift it. I often felt that after lifting it… before even hitting it, I knew it was going over because my lift was proper. Other days you might lift it arse-ways and you'd struggle to get your hands back, or your hurley back on it, to give it direction. Particularly back then, when the rim on the ball could play havoc with you.

You mightn't see a new ball for 20 minutes in a match. You could be belting the same ball around… and that's where Cusack thought he was being clever with the bag of sliotars.

Our doctor Tom Higgins came to us the Wednesday night before the match, and said, 'By the way lads, the GAA have brought in drug testing and ye could be called on Sunday'.

I had asthma and I had a Ventolin inhaler, and that was on the banned list if you took too much of it. Too much coffee was on the list, and alcohol. So, we hadn't a clue.

If you were on medication from your doctor for your chest, or for a cold or anything, Benylin Plus or Nurofen Plus, you could be hauled in… *take a wee in a jar and be the first GAA player ever to be suspended.*

So, we decided, 'No, we're not!'

Brian Flannery and myself were the two lads picked in a blind ballot by all accounts. There was contact made with the Cork team and they said no as well. Fergal Ryan and Ben O'Connor were called from Cork and I know Fergal well, and he kicked up, but Frank Murphy got them to go. Our chairman Paddy Joe Ryan was having a hernia.

There was a bit of argy-bargy. Al Guy from the Irish Sports Council wasn't allowed in, as far as I can remember. We wouldn't let him in. Paul Kelly and Roger

Casey used to be with us doing the hurleys and the gear, and Paul stood guard at the door and didn't let anyone in! RTÉ made a thing of nothing about it and, all of a sudden, it was a story and then we just had to get on with it and do it.

We left and we went down to the hotel; there was word then that Cork were going to claim the match. So, we agreed to do it in the hotel. Al Guy tested us in the Anner Hotel and we were clean obviously.

If you're going to do a drug test, educate the people and let them know what's allowed and what's not allowed. That's nearly 20 years ago… you could get caught with Benylin or Aspirin, you just wouldn't know and the implications socially and professionally for anyone could be massive.

My relationship with Justin was very good. Justin was his own man. A very opinionated man about hurling. Very knowledgeable about the skills of the game. He didn't worry too much about the opposition, which was something I found very good.

There was no such thing as, we'll change our ways to stymie the opposition. *We'll set our own stall out and we'll go and play.* Obviously, the modern game is completely different to that! There were occasions when we got caught. Generally, we tried to go toe-to-toe with other teams and play as best we could.

He had a great emphasis on the speed of your hands and the strength of your wrists. There's a couple of sides to coaching. Skills coaching… he was very good. Positional coaching… he trusted the players. I think a coach that trusts his players is way ahead of his time rather than trying to bombard players with information about how to play.

He trusted you once you had skills, initiative and a hurling brain.

Obviously, there would be days when that didn't happen. In general, it wasn't a load of instructions… or X, Y, Z. Once you were hurling fit and hurling ready, he trusted the players to go with their instincts.

He never doubted the players' instincts. That was his strongest suit.

It was tough love with my father Pat.

When he was charge of our own teams in Ballygunner growing up, you wouldn't get any favouritism or anything like that. He was competitive to the point where developing players was more important to him than the result in the early days in the juvenile club in Ballygunner.

I'd chat to him, I'd ask him for advice; he'd see things from the stand that needed addressing or he'd notice something about the corner-backs or wing backs. He was a sounding board every time I needed a sounding board. But praise was a very hard thing to get. You wouldn't be talking to him seeking praise, it was more of an open discussion.

The longer it went on the more you think you know yourself, but it's always good to have someone you can rely on who has your best interests at heart. He never gloated. He played himself; they had an unlucky few years when he played.

It would have been nice if we got to a final when we were all in our prime, maybe 2002 or '04, and see how that would have went for us. My father was a very proud Waterford man and a very proud Ballygunner man.

He drove the bus for a couple of years under Gerald McCarthy. He had a good, strong friendships with a lot of lads on the team. A couple of lads would have asked his opinion when he was driving the bus and stuff like that. It was nice to have that. I hope we win an All-Ireland. The sooner the better to get us off and running. For the young people in the county to see Waterford winning one… if you see someone winning one in your own locality or your own parish, you have something to aim for as a young player. That's the most important thing.

I would have taken getting to two finals in my prime, and taking my chances with that rather than any individual awards. My first five years for Waterford, we didn't win a championship match… 1993 to '97. We went down to Kerry, after being beaten in the league final in 1998, and, only for we bucked up in the last five minutes, we could have been dumped out of the championship down in Tralee… but then we beat Tipperary in Cork. The knockout fashion of hurling was brilliant and it was cruel, but that's the way it was. If you won a match, you could get on a run. If you got a bit of bad luck and lost a match, there'd be no run.

BRIAN GREENE
(FERGAL HARTLEY & JOHN MULLANE)

WATERFORD 2-23 TIPPERARY 3-12
Munster SHC Final
Páirc Uí Chaoimh
JUNE 30, 2002

Brian Greene walks off the field after Waterford defeated Tipperary and captured the Munster title in Páirc Uí Chaoimh (and celebrates with the trophy), as ghosts of generations past rest happily.

★ **WATERFORD:** S Brenner; B Flannery, T Feeney, **B Greene**; E Murphy, **F Hartley**, P Queally; T Browne (1-0), J Murray; E Kelly (0-3), S Prendergast (0-1), P Flynn (1-6); **J Mullane (0-4)**, K McGrath (0-7), E McGrath (0-1). Subs: D Bennett (0-1) for Flannery, M White for Flynn, A Moloney for Prendergast, D Shanahan for E McGrath.

★ **TIPPERARY:** B Cummins; T Costelloe, P Maher, D Fahey; E Corcoran, D Kennedy, P Kelly; T Dunne (0-2), N Morris; B O'Meara, C Gleeson (0-2), B Dunne (2-2); E Kelly (1-4), J Carroll (0-1), L Corbett (0-1). Subs: E Enright for Morris, P Ormonde for Kennedy, M O'Leary for Costelloe, P O'Brien for Gleeson.

THE ACTION

'THE REAL FAMINE is over,' proclaimed Déise captain Fergal Hartley, in front of President Mary McAleese, as he raised the Munster cup aloft. Waterford waited 39 years for this day to arrive.

Justin McCarthy's men went in as rank outsiders against the 2001 All-Ireland champions. Former Tipp boss Babs Keating claimed that the Premier County would prevail by 10 points in one newspaper that morning.

On the day that Brazil won the World Cup, Waterford played Samba hurling. The men in white and blue should have won by a bigger margin. They hit 11 second-half wides and 17 in total.

McCarthy brought in 1959 All-Ireland winners Frankie Walsh, Tom Cheasty and Martin Óg Morrissey to speak to the team at training on the Thursday night. The older generation inspired new heroes to emerge. It was Ken McGrath's greatest display in a white and blue shirt. The Man of the Match shot seven points from play at centre-forward.

The Mount Sion master was supported up front by new kids on the block; Eoin Kelly, John Mullane and McGrath's younger brother Eoin.

The underdogs took a gamble by playing against the breeze in the first-half. It paid off as they only trailed by a point at the change of ends (1-10 to 1-9). Paul Flynn blasted a trademark close range free to the net past Brendan Cummins and four Tipperary defenders in the 17th minute. Eoin Kelly did likewise at the other end in first-half injury-time.

A double blast from Benny Dunne left the sides all square on 46 minutes (3-10 to 1-16) but Waterford weren't to be denied. Tony Browne raced onto a booming Stephen Brenner free on 53 minutes and whipped to the net. White flags followed from Ken McGrath, John Mullane and Seamus Prendergast and Waterford were out of sight.

★ ★ ★ ★ ★

"

I KNOW THERE are fellas out there with loads of Munster medals… Leinster medals, All-Ireland medals… you name it, but I don't think they could understand how I felt about 2002.

I was born in 1970. At the time, my father was playing hurling with Waterford. As soon as I was old enough to walk, I was carted along to every challenge match, every league match and every championship match! I was in the dressing-room a thousand times with the likes of my father, John Galvin, Mossie Walsh, Pat McGrath, Tom Casey, Seamie Hannon… all these great men.

I had a little personal relationship with each and every one of them. By the time Waterford hurling came back in the early 80s, I was a young impressionable lad of about 12 years of age. My father had played for years with the county in the 70s and when it got to the 80s, he was slipping into his thirties. Joe McGrath came into the county and there was a huge amount of work my father had to do; he must have lost three or four stone and got back very fit. I saw all of that… all of that effort.

I never wanted to do anything other than hurl for Waterford. My father was after getting an All Star and I was asked what did I want? I said I wanted two All Stars! To go one better! The dreams of a 12-year-old boy!

When Waterford did eventually get to the Munster final, I had seen what my father and all the lads had gone through. My father was getting collected to go training or he would be driving; all the boys would come in and meet in the white house. You might have Pat McGrath, Pat Ryan or other lads getting collected. There was a huge amount of excitement leading up to it and I was after seeing the huge effort my father was after putting into it.

It was a magical time for Waterford hurling and it was a magical time to be living in my house, and it was a *magical time* to have a father who was an All Star. It was wonderful.

I remember watching the two Munster finals and my father played well in the two of them. He was red-hot at the time. *The feeling of disappointment.* I was normally in the stand with my mother, with all the families, but I happened to be up in the terrace for the first final. I was after going on the school bus as you do when you get old enough.

I remember the feeling of watching my father walking off the field. I was always an emotional fella and I'd feel that in my stomach. I'd feel that disappointment for him. The following year in Limerick, the same thing… I felt that again. After that, a Munster final to me was like the Holy Grail.

I played in two Munster finals in 1998 and came out on the wrong side of both. In the first game, Jamesie O'Connor handed me my backside! You know what I mean. In the second game, I handed him his backside, but they won. It was bittersweet.

The Munster final was like this insurmountable wall in my family's' existence. My grandfather has one since 1938 and after that my father, his brother, me… *following it was such an insurmountable thing*. This was my Holy Grail.

The morning of the match in 2002, I went over to Ferrybank, to the graveyard. My grandfather is buried there.

I picked a stone off the grave, a little marble stone, and I brought it home with me. I was getting the gear ready, throwing the gear in the bag. You know where the lace goes into the shorts… I got the stone into the shorts! Going down to the field that day, after being in Munster finals in 1998 and watching my father in the early 80s, there was an awful lot I had riding on it personally… emotionally, you know what I mean.

All of a sudden, the first-half happens. It didn't go all my own way now. I was marking Eoin Kelly and he was the new kid on the block at the time. I was in my early thirties. I didn't go well.

In fairness, the ball he got in the first-half, I'll never forget it.

I was flying, I was in good shape but he was a tremendously hard hurler to deal with. With the type of ball that was coming into him, I really hadn't a hope. The actual supply of ball in the first-half to the Tipperary forward line was crippling us. We talked about it at half-time and the second-half began and… my God! It was almost like we came up on a crest of a wave.

I remember looking at Nicky English before the game. He was the Tipperary manager that day. I would have met Nicky a couple of times, he would have been on All Star trips with my father. I lived in Tipp town for a year when I started playing with Waterford first. He was from Golden, so I ran across him a couple of times.

When I was a young fella, 19 or 20, I was drunk one night and I told Nicky that I would hurl *this* off him and hurl *that* off him! *As you would!* Making an eejit of myself, of course!

We had made up our minds that day.

Clare had this thing that they wouldn't be the whipping boys of Munster. We decided as a group that day… that… *This was it!* It was all or nothing.

There are times in your life where you draw a line in the sand here, there… *everywhere.* We had enough lines drawn in the sand. We were boxed in. There was only one way to go and that was to break out.

About five or 10 minutes into the second-half, this thing took on a different life. Slowly but surely, it was like someone was washing the muck off us after years and years of being downtrodden. Everything was clearer.

Formula 1 drivers talk about the perfect lap; we were in the middle of it, we knew it was happening, we nearly couldn't believe it. There was a part of you saying… *Is this what it feels like?* To see the Tipperary lads… *We are dealing with the All-Ireland champions here, they just can't handle it.*

There's an old thing in Mount Sion years ago called the Mount Sion spirit. It comes from the team that won nine in-a -row in the 50s. A hundred times I heard Pat Fanning describing it. Every time he described it, it was something else.

That man could pick words. He was a different type of individual.

We had this Mount Sion spirit and I remember feeling that… playing on a team with my father, Pat McGrath and getting my first championship when I was only 17. I remember feeling that spirit that they talked about. It's a refusal lie down, a stubbornness.

This was happening with Waterford. This wasn't happening in Walsh Park, this wasn't happening in Fraher Field, this was happening on the big stage.

For that to happen and to see the lads growing into it… amazing.

We were under pressure in the defence and Tipperary pushed and *pushed* but we seemed to raise our game then. We just seemed to come out in the second-half a different team.

I don't know were we more relaxed or more focused, *I'm not too sure.*

To be part of that, I mean I almost felt like a spectator in the back line!

I don't have a great memory of what happened in the game but what sticks out in my mind is how hard Kelly was to deal with in the first-half. I never really thought I was after doing alright. You'd be talking to fellas… *Jesus Greener do you remember 2002? You had some game lad'.* Everyone would tell you that.

They mightn't have been at the game and someone would still tell you that! Looking back on it, I didn't think I was after doing alright. Delighted that we won, don't get me wrong, but I didn't think I was after doing alright.

It was only looking back on it, years after, and watching bits of the game here and there, it brings it all back to you. Slowly but surely, I felt over the years that I was after doing alright in the second-half! I did grand, I did exactly what I wanted to do in the second-half.

I didn't give him a sniff.

I went over a Tipp lad's head to tap down a ball and the ball came down and bounced. I tapped down the ball and the referee blew his whistle. Tony Browne came in and took the ball. I couldn't believe it for a second.

I actually turned to the referee and put my hands out… 'What was that for?'

I thought he was blowing me for a free.

That one little bit of the whistle turned into the second part and then the third part that finishes the game. As the second and the third whistle came out, I never in my life felt anything like that. It was a realisation of a life's dream. I had watched my father and I had seen what it meant to him. After everything, here I was in my early thirties, on the field and we had just won a Munster final… *we just won, like.*

I was just overcome. I remember dropping to my knees.

My hands weren't even on my head, my hands were limp. I was limp.

Every bit of me was so relieved. It was like a generation of relief, if you understand me. It means more to other people and less to other people. To me, I was going to die a happy man now. No matter what happened after that day… and there's some great things after happening me since, but right there and then, I felt ghosts leaving my body. It was the perfect way to win a Munster final.

It was emphatic; we were brushing people aside, and the out-pouring of emotion, I'll never forget it. My good friend Micheal White, the two of us would have been very pally at the time, he knew what it was all about because we were wicked tight. He was the first to get out to me, and then Eoin Kelly.

There's a picture of the three of us down on our knees, I have it hanging by the stairs at home. That feeling was just phenomenal. It was like every little thing you cared about all your life was after coming true. We got over the line and when I say we… I'm talking about Waterford, I'm talking about me and my friends, Tony, Ken, Hartley and also my family personally.

When I did get up off the ground, obviously the first person I wanted to look for was the big fella! When we did meet each other that was special.

I felt like I was realising *his* dream.

I know what that meant to him. I know my daddy and I saw his body language leaving the field in the early 80s. I knew what it meant to him then, and here I was after getting across the line. To see him then, and to catch eyes… I get teary-eyed now even thinking about it.

We played Tipp in the Munster Championship in 1995 and there was a big row. No one got sent off but there was talk about it on *The Sunday Game* that night. Eventually, a few of us got pulled up in front of the Munster Council. I got a month, Peter Queally got two months and I think three of the Tipp lads got something as well. After we had been beaten.

I slipped away then.

I got a call. Pat Walsh from The Nire was heading out to America and they were looking for someone. I wasn't working at the time. I went for a weekend. The game was a draw and I said that I'd stay a week or two, and save them another ticket and get a bit of work; I was a carpenter.

They did that. I stayed two years that time!

I did well over there. I played for New York a couple of times and I won a New York Senior Championship over there with Westmeath actually! In 1996, I came back and played in the Connacht Championship against Galway. In 1995, we played against Derry out in New York in the Ulster Championship. I was getting onto the father that I played in three different championships!

I came back in 1997, but I suffered a hamstring injury. That was Gerald McCarthy's first year. I was struggling to get fit. Then 1998 happened. In 1999, we got beaten by Cork. Micheal White was mad to go to America. James Murray was already out there with a lad from Carrick, so Haulie wanted to go out.

I made the call. I was after getting stopped in 1997 on the way back from New York, so I was after getting a ban. I rang Richie Comerford from St Mollerans, he was the manager.

I spent two years out in Chicago. I had a good time; I won a North American Senior Championship with Harry Bolands. I played with Alan Markham from Clare, Martin 'Gorta' Comerford from Kilkenny and Brian Geary from Limerick.

I came back from there and I went back to New York for the last year. Pat Ryan was involved up in Stanford. I lived in Stanford back in 1995 and '96 but they hadn't a hurling team. They had a junior team now, so they looked after me and set me up in an apartment and I drove over in a U-Haul van… myself and Debbie.

We won a New York Junior Championship that year. I definitely thought at that stage that was the end of my inter-county career. I was after winning a New York Junior Championship medal… that's where I was at, you know what I mean.

Then 9/11 happened that year. We were living in Stanford, about 25 miles outside New York. I was working in New York.

The place changed over there. Myself and Debbie were in our early thirties and we were thinking about starting a family. That put a spanner in the works. We decided that we didn't want to raise children there and that we'd head home.

Actually, Ken McGrath and Henry Shefflin got stuck out there! They stayed up with myself and Pat Ryan one of the nights!

Bonnie Kennedy used to hurl with Tipp underage; he had a gym out there. I remember I used to jog about five miles over to their place to the gym and jog back. A Tipp player prepared me for what was to come in 2002!

I was talking to my father and he was taking the Mount Sion job again.

I was actually talking to Justin as well. Justin said that he'd give me a shot. The first training I went to was county training when I came home.

I was delighted to get home in the end; I came home just before St Patrick's weekend. I got my chance then. I was still struggling with the hamstring. Ken was injured as well.

Then, the two of us were brought on towards the end of the Cork game and it just happened for us. I remember going on and McCarthy just said, 'Run at them!'

He put me on right half-forward. At one stage, I followed a midfielder to the right corner-back position and got in a hook and the ball was driven wide. I was only on the field 10 minutes.

I was very lucky to be on some really good teams. Maybe if I did things differently, myself personally, I could have stepped up another rung or two on the ladder. It's easy to look back and say that. It's hard to put an old head on young shoulders sometimes.

I remember going out the tunnel in 2002, and I met Stephen Frampton. I remember telling him, 'This one is for you!'

I meant every bit of that.

He should have never been put off the panel.

I still have the jersey, the No 7. I was playing corner-back that day but seven would be my lucky number.

The first senior championship I won with Mount Sion, I have the jersey from that. I wasn't playing that day, Pat Ryan was playing No 7. I was after doing my collarbone the week before.

Pat came up to the house that evening and he gave me the jersey... No 7. He reckoned that I was after earning it, I was No 7 for the majority of the year. I have that. I lost the stone. I never found the stone after.

It's an honour to be a Greene, and that day more than ever.

There were a lot of ghosts released that day and went to heaven happy people. I was so lucky to be part and parcel of that team and play with the individuals I played with down through the years.

We carried them with us on that day.

We were just very lucky to be in the Waterford jersey that day, and any of the lads you talk to will tell you the same thing.

FERGAL HARTLEY

Fergal Hartley leads his team around the field in Páirc Uí Chaoimh before the Munster final in 2002 and (inset) raises the Munster trophy high in the air.

❝

YOU CAN'T FAKE belief; you have to really believe.

Most teams go out telling themselves they can do it, but they don't really believe they... *can do it.* And if you don't really believe you can do it and the shit hits the fan, that's when you get in trouble. The shit did hit the fan that day, particularly when Benny Dunne got the third goal. You have to *really believe* at that stage. If you don't believe at that point, that you're going to win this game... you're gone!

On the week of a match, I'd often score players out of 10. Ours and theirs.

Obviously, you'd have a bias towards your own. Individual players, then a total for the Waterford team and a total for the opposition. It's like something you do when you're a kid!

I used to try and do it honestly for myself, so I could actually stand over it and say… *Yeah I really believe this!* You have to convince yourself to some extent but the convincing yourself has to be real. If it's not real then you're not really *convincing* yourself; you're telling yourself, but not convincing yourself.

That's the process I used to go through and that Munster final was the first time I ever shared it with a team… any team, club or county. My point was, I firmly believe we're going to win this game. We say it every day, we can't ever go out and say we're not going to win; every team does that, no matter how unrealistic it is.

Coming away from training that week, and particularly that meeting in Mount Sion on the Friday night, I felt that everybody felt it. Everybody felt that we were going to win this game and it's going to take a mammoth Tipperary performance, as All-Ireland champions, to beat us. *If this is any way close, we're going to win it.*

The second thing I used to do was, I would compare our centre-back to their centre-back, and our centre-forward to their centre-forward and then think… *How many battles are we going to win?* I did it every which way.

I did every combination and I worked it out. I knew the players we had, with the likes of Tom Feeney at full-back. Philip Maher was seen as the best full-back in the country but I felt, if I was picking my best team in the morning, I'd want Tom Feeney on my team.

When you can say that honestly to yourself, it actually gives you great belief. I remember sharing this with the team in the meeting the night before the match, on the basis of saying I actually, genuinely believe we are superior to them. You have to have a basis for your belief and this was the basis for my belief.

I felt, going through that team, outside of Tommy Dunne and Eoin Kelly, their big stars… *Who else have we to worry about?*

Who else on their team would we want on our team? When you get to the point of when the shit hits the fan, particularly when the game is there to be won, which is usually in the second-half, that's when that deep belief kicks in.

That was the reason we won the game.

When Benny Dunne got that goal, ordinarily when you're All-Ireland champions and ordinarily when the other team are usually the also-rans… usually the team that goes for the moral victory rather than the real victory… that's the time when the tide turns and that's the time when the All-Ireland champions kick on.

And the underdog thinks... *Okay, our time is up here!...* and they raise the white flag.

When you're playing a game, self-talk goes on in your head. It's continuous self-talk. I remember, after Benny Dunne's goal, I was saying to myself... *This is not the end... this ain't happening.* I felt really confident that everyone else was feeling the same even though we had been hit with a sucker punch.

In my head, the goal was kind of against the run of play. At that point, we were probably the better team. Ordinarily, in the past, that was the time Waterford said... *We're up against it here now, we'll do our best but we've no expectations of winning.* In my head, it was different that day. I felt it, and I felt the whole team felt it.

It's one thing you feeling it yourself but you have to know that the rest of the team are feeling it as well. I don't know how you quantify that, I don't know how you capture that, but you do in a team; you know by the body language, you know by the next ball, the communication. You know whether heads are down or whether heads are up. You just know it... *you sense it.* The sense there was I knew this wasn't the end for me and I just knew everyone else was feeling the same.

That's the point where it would have turned against us normally. Justin McCarthy was a big part of it, in the belief he brought to the team and the belief he had in himself. I was confident we were the better team and that's where the deep belief comes in, not the shallow confidence that you talk about but you don't really have.

The Antrim trip is a big part of the story.

From what was a huge negative within the panel, it turned out to be a massive positive. Nobody wanted to go. It was two weeks before the Cork game and we felt that we should have been playing a first-tier team. That was the general consensus of the senior players in the team, and I approached Justin.

Justin was a man who knew what he wanted. We were going to Antrim and that was it! Some aspects of the trip to Antrim were almost catastrophic to some extent! But it ended up being a fantastic weekend for all the wrong reasons!

It was nearly midnight when we arrived up there. We met and had our breakfast that morning around eleven o'clock and got the train around one o'clock from Waterford to Dublin. Then, we got a bus from Dublin.

We were travelling for 10 or 11 hours. Players were hungry and getting irate. We arrived up there around half eleven and, as always when we were in Antrim or Down, we got a huge feed. We finished eating this food around midnight or after… a festival of food, it was superb!

We went out for a walk in the fresh air. There was an old woman sweeping out a pub and she was about to close up. We had a bit of a conflab, a mini-huddle. Some players said, 'Will we go for a drink and get this out of our system?'

Between the jigs and the reels, we said we'd go in and have two drinks and go to bed; help us to sleep, because we weren't going to sleep after this big feed. Those two drinks didn't go to plan as can sometimes happen when you put 30 lads inside a small pub! We got out of there about five o'clock in the morning!

After having a whale of a time, everyone knew the next morning that this wasn't what we should have done. Obviously, nobody was saying anything to Justin about what went on the night before; we were all looking at each other a bit sheepishly! But there was a bit of spirit about us because we were after having great craic the night before.

We knew we weren't well prepared to play Antrim, but we played great hurling albeit we were suffering a little bit! After that, Justin said, 'If you want to have a couple of pints, you can have a couple of pints!' Effectively, we had a second night on the beer! It wasn't what we were expecting for the weekend!

I remember coming back on the train on the Sunday and we had a players' meeting and we said, 'Lads, look… we're after having an absolutely fantastic weekend, not by design but by accident'. The spirit coming back from Antrim that day, albeit we all knew we were after doing the wrong thing; there was a bond, there was a gel, there was a spirit that came from us all socialising together, from us all being together for the one weekend and being in a situation which was a sub-optimal situation, and we turned it into something special. The spirit coming down on that train was something I hadn't experienced in a team before.

Training on Tuesday night was electric. Everything was perfect. Every player knew now it was time to put the shoulder to the wheel and, suddenly, a spirit began to build which hadn't been there prior to that weekend.

We built a bit of confidence in ourselves because we knew there was something special happening.

I was 30 years of age.

In my early days, if we were written off, as we often would have been, that would have played on my mind. Whereas in my latter years, as I got older, I used to love the notion of being written off because it would motivate me. Something in the paper, particularly if it came from an opposition manager or player... if you remember the Babs Keating headlines.

Maybe in the past, when I was younger, somewhere along the way that would play on my mind. *Is he right? Is there some substance in what he's saying?* As you get older, you're able to process that differently and you have enough belief in yourself to *process* that differently. Sure, everyone was writing us off because Tipp were such red-hot favourites.

Even against Cork, we were being written off because we were missing Ken McGrath and Brian Greene that day. Ken was our talisman and we weren't given a chance without Ken. I loved it. Every time I read it, it was in the locker, in the locker every time. Just to give myself that burning motivation if you like.

We met President Mary McAleese that day and ordinarily, that should be a great honour. I remember, everyone was in the same boat, we just weren't interested. That's not meant in any disrespectful way to the President, it just wasn't what we were there for.

It's a funny one because, ordinarily, you'd be very proud to lead your team and introduce them all to the President but all I could think of was, 'Let's get this over with, we want to get on with business here. We're not here to shake hands with the President'.

I think that was the general sense in the team. I don't want that to come across as disrespectful because it isn't meant that way. We were so focussed on what we wanted to do. These were all just distractions.

'Let's get this thing done, let's get it out of the way.'

You should be going up with a smile on your face meeting the President; I just wanted this thing done and out of the way. It was the exact same for all the players. You could see it in lads' eyes.

'Get me out there, I want this ball to be thrown in.'

It's hard to put words on it; it's hard to explain the ecstasy. I went over to my good wife Fiona; we were expecting our first child at the time, our eldest daughter Lauren. I had forgotten all about the fact that I had to do a speech!

I'm not superstitious but I wouldn't ever, for club or county, prepare a post-match speech. It's almost like tempting fate. I don't know why, I just felt uncomfortable doing it. I just felt... *Jesus you're putting the cart before the horse big-time here.* Focus on the game not what you're going to say.

Ordinarily, that should have been a period where I should have got my head together and start thinking about what I'm going to say. I nearly forgot about that. Someone grabbed me by the arm and said, 'You've got to go up!' Even while I was going across, literally I was on top of the steps thinking... *Oh no, what do I say now?* I don't know what words you would use to describe it, particularly when we were waiting so long.

At 30 years of age you're asking the question... *Will I ever see this in my time?*

It was different for the Eoin Kellys and the John Mullanes, who were at the start of their careers. When you've been through the mill and been on the receiving end of the wrong results so many times, you would be questioning... *Is this ever going to happen?*

And then for it to happen for myself and the older lads, the likes of Peter Queally, Brian Greene and so on. For lads like us, who had been around the block, it was almost unbelievable.

We were blown away by the receptions in Dungarvan and Waterford both days. No matter where you'd go, you'd get a taxi and the taxi wouldn't charge you. You'd go into a pub and you could barely buy a pint. You'd barely get to the counter. Someone would either buy it for you or the barman would give it to you for nothing.

There couldn't have been more goodwill.

I retired for work reasons in 2003.

I was thinking in my head... *This is going to be my last year.* That narrative starts when you're around 30. It's not just in your own head but people are asking you, 'Are you going to play another year' and all that kind of stuff. It almost becomes... Why are they asking me this? Like, I felt as good as I ever felt, yet to be asked this question, 'Will you go another year?'

I went and I retired... and I went back!

I missed out on 2004 which was a regret. I don't have too many regrets but that would be one. I felt I was still fit enough and I was still young enough, and yet I retired. Hindsight is a great thing but it was a bad decision at the time.

It was a huge honour to win an All Star in 2002, particularly given that Waterford didn't have a huge amount of All Stars at that stage. We only had five… John Galvin, Jim Greene, Mossie Walsh and Tony Browne. John Galvin had two. It was a huge honour. It was a great end to the year.

My daughter Lauren was born on September 17; I got an All Star and I captained Waterford to win Munster for the first time in 39 years.

It was the perfect year.

JOHN MULLANE

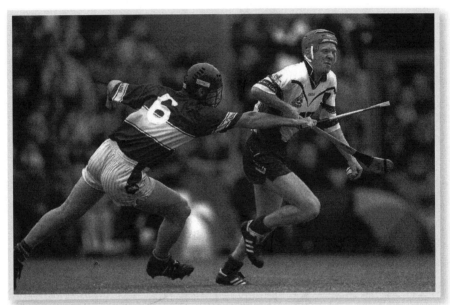

John Mullane bursts past the challenge of David Kennedy of Tipperary in the epic breakthrough 2002 Munster final in Páirc Uí Chaoimh.

66

MYSELF AND BRIAN 'Bull' Phelan won five grand between the two of us on the morning of the Munster final. Jesus, it was unbelievable.

We both backed Ronaldo to be top goal-scorer and Brazil to win the World Cup, and we did the double as well. We were getting the food in Lawlors Hotel… the pasta and the chicken, and the World Cup final happened to be on at the same time.

Ronaldo got the first goal and the second goal… and Brazil ended up winning 2-0. I turned around to 'Bull' and I said, 'Jesus, this could be the start of an unbelievable day!'

I don't really remember too much after that.

I remember it was raining and we went down to Midleton GAA club for a puck-around. The day just went so quick. What I really, really remember was Fergal Hartley's speech in the dressing-room; it was probably the best speech I ever heard from a captain and I've been in dressing-rooms over the years with Brick Walsh, Tony Browne and Ken McGrath… and even in my own club.

The speech he gave that day was just unbelievable.

There wasn't a pin dropping in the dressing-room. You could see the emotion on lads' faces. We weren't going to be beaten that day after that speech.

He was talking about family, what it meant to the Waterford people.

He remarked on the 39 years… loved ones that weren't with us, people that had passed away who were great lovers of Waterford over the years… *it was as much for them.*

The famine had to end and we weren't going to come off that field beaten.

It just resonated with the whole dressing-room. I was a young fella in there with Eoin McGrath, Seamus Prendergast and Eoin Kelly. We were all new on the scene. He remarked on 1998… the anguish of '98, it was just an unbelievable speech and I *knew* by the speech.

I'll be straight with you, I was privileged to be even in a dressing-room with the likes of Hartley, Browne, Ken McGrath, Paul Flynn and Dan Shanahan, because they were my heroes of 1998. Those were lads who inspired me to go on, to be ambitious and to try and break into the Waterford team and hopefully play in a Munster final.

I was living the dream really. Once the speech was over, I knew we weren't going to be beaten. You know when you get a sense that something is going to happen? You can gauge by the atmosphere in the dressing-room.

The pitch of the atmosphere in the room that day after Fergal Hartley's speech was just perfect to go out and tear into Tipp.

I didn't think it would happen so fast for me, to tell you the truth, because I was very lightweight. I had an awful lot of speed and back then it was very hard for a newcomer coming in from a lesser club. De La Salle back then, we were a small club in contrast to where we are today.

It was always going to be very hard to break into a set-up, let alone break into a starting fifteen. Gerald McCarthy, to be fair to him, gave me my break and sometimes you need to get a break. Gerald McCarthy had the trust in me… Damian Byrne, Mick Gaffney and Declan Fitzpatrick were the selectors. They believed that I was good enough to push on for Waterford.

Who was very good to me and he's passed away since, was Jim Dee the Waterford team secretary. It was one of the most beautiful things that Jim did for me.

I'll never ever forget it.

We were playing WIT out in Fenor and I was travelling with Stevie Brenner and I was only a newcomer, and I was afraid to ask fellas for a lift. I had no lift out to Fenor; Stevie couldn't collect me.

The other city lads… the cars were full.

I said, 'Jesus, will I bother going out or will I leave it off?'

I rang Jim Dee and I said, 'Look, I've no lift out… I don't know will I bother going.' I was a bit nervous going into a new set-up. Lo and behold, Jim Dee said, 'You won't… I'll come down and collect you'.

He came down from Dungarvan, collected me and brought me out to Fenor, and I never looked back after that moment really. It was just such a lovely thing to do. It gave me the security that lads were willing to do things like that and lads had your back. I built up a great relationship with Jim in the aftermath. I never looked back from that moment. It was something I never, ever forgot.

There's moments you look back on in your career and that was just one moment where I was able to reflect back and say it was such a lovely thing to do at that time.

The fans weren't allowed out onto the pitch that year and out of the corner of my eye, a couple of lads I knew… Parish Power and Colin Morrissey, they were Mount Sion lads but really good lads, real hardcore Waterford supporters. Lads who I would have been on the terrace with in 1998, because I was on the terrace with the fans in '98… *the summer of '98 was just epic.*

I could resonate with how they were feeling in the aftermath, the tears and the joy. We were finally after getting over the line and I thought… *I'm just going to go for it.* I went to the railing and there was Parish Power and Colin Morrissey on top of the railing, and Eoin McGrath followed me… jumping up on the railing. We went bonkers really!

I just felt… *You know what, I'm really going to enjoy this moment.*

Unfortunately, I threw my jersey into the crowd! I got caught up in it a bit too much! Who actually got my jersey was Kieran O'Toole, the referee! I didn't know him at the time.

It got out that that I was looking for my jersey back, it was my first Munster final and I wanted to hang onto the jersey. Kieran rang me and he said, 'I have your jersey!'

I called over to the house and knocked on the door and I said, 'Can I have my jersey?' and he told me, 'Go away from the door… you have the wrong house!'

Then, he said, 'No… I'm only messing… COME IN, COME IN.'

He brought me in anyway and we even had a drink in the house and he gave me back the jersey. That was the week of it.

Going back to the Imperial Hotel in Cork and to see what it meant to the supporters… they were all back there. It was just unbelievable.

I remember Seán Cullinane was on the bus. I kind of felt half-guilty; I was lucky really, I was only starting off in the panel a wet day and there were others like Brendan Landers, Stephen Frampton… and Sean Cullinane, who left the panel in March just before the championship kicked in.

I really, really thought of those lads when we won it because there was me winning a Munster Championship and these lads had given 14 or 15 years to the Waterford jersey, they were just so unlucky to miss out. I'll never forget The Rock was on the bus on the way back and it would have been hard on him, but he knew what it meant to Waterford and he enjoyed the journey.

Peter Queally had the cup and he went into Youghal garda station. He was stationed in Youghal at the time. And then, the bus driver Billy Costine stopped the bus and we walked over Youghal bridge. That was an incredible moment. For the first time in 39 years, we were bringing silverware back into the county.

I can still relive that to this day. Then, into Dungarvan, we didn't really know what to expect. What awaited us in Dungarvan was just unbelievable.

I ended up sleeping in James Murray's bath that night; there was bodies everywhere! James Murray was living in a housing estate in Dungarvan… there must have been about 40 or 50 people in his house! All the bedrooms were locked! Murray was cute enough, he locked up all the bedrooms!

The only place I could crash down was the bath! So, I ended up sleeping in the bath!

Woke up the next morning! Owen Dermody was the bookie… and myself and the Bull went down to him. Five grand between the two of us. I remember being down in the Showboat pub and I was buying everyone drink there! There were fellas I didn't even know and I was buying them a drink! The Showboat were good now, they were giving out free drink, but I must have spent a thousand euro on drink. I was just in the moment like.

I think it was two grand I had left and Bull had two. I remember talking to Leon Tracey. 'Look, I'll be back to collect the other two at the end of the week.'

I spent about a thousand euro on buying people drink. Then, we went onto the bus down the quay. It was an unbelievable week, the stuff of dreams really.

It didn't help us going into an All-Ireland semi-final. I think it was six weeks we had to wait for the semi-final. If we didn't win that Munster final, it probably could have gone the other way, and we mightn't have had the success we had in the noughties.

We probably mightn't have pushed on and won the other Munster titles. When you win one, the monkey is off the back and you believe… *We can win another one!* It probably set Waterford up for what was to come really. Look at the success they had winning minor and under-21, and an awful lot of those young fellas would have been watching our team.

Our generation inspired an awful lot of those young lads to push on and want to play hurling for Waterford, and want to win for Waterford. That's the way it is, it's like a cycle really. The lads nowadays are going to inspire another generation. For me, they were magical times, magical moments and it was great to be a part of and to share those moments with great lads.

Next year is the 20th anniversary of that great win and, hopefully, we can get together and have a night and reflect on what was a fantastic day.

It will always beat me up that we didn't win an All-Ireland.

I always find it difficult in and around the All-Ireland final weekend that we didn't get over the line because I think we had the team to get over the line. Unfortunately, we ran into a very good Cork team and a very good Kilkenny team at the time. If we were playing in any other era, we probably would have got over the line. We just couldn't get the logistics of the Dublin thing right. It wasn't Croke Park, it was more the logistics as regards the travel at the time. We tried everything... flying up, going on the train, staying in different hotels... we just couldn't get the logistics right for Croke Park.

If the All-Ireland series was played in Thurles, I think we would have got over the line. Look, we had enough opportunities at it and we just fell short in the end.

When I reflect, I wouldn't give the 12 years up for anything, particularly in the noughties and particularly to be a Waterford player playing in that era.

The height of the Celtic Tiger, playing in front of 40,000 or 50,000 people the majority of the days you went out in the championship. We went on some fabulous training camps and some fabulous trips as well, days that I will look back on and know... it was a great time to be a Waterford hurler.

KEN McGRATH

WATERFORD 3-16 CORK 1-21
Munster SHC Final
Semple Stadium
JUNE 27, 2004

Ken McGrath (right) is pictured with Waterford teammates Paul Flynn and Dan Shanahan when they were chosen as All Stars to honour their performances in the summer of 2004.

★ **WATERFORD:** S Brenner; J Murray, D Prendergast, E Murphy; T Browne, **K McGrath (0-1)**, B Phelan; E Kelly (1-1), D Bennett (0-1); D Shanahan (1-3), M Walsh, P Flynn (1-7); J Mullane (0-2), S Prendergast (0-1), E McGrath. Subs: P O'Brien for Bennett, S O'Sullivan for E McGrath, J Kennedy for O'Brien.

★ **CORK:** D Óg Cusack; W Sherlock, D O'Sullivan, B Murphy; S Óg Ó hAilpín, R Curran (0-1), J Gardiner; T Kenny (0-3), J O'Connor (0-2); G McCarthy (1-0), N McCarthy, T McCarthy; B O'Connor (0-4), B Corcoran (0-2), J Deane (0-9). Subs: J O'Callaghan for N McCarthy, K Murphy for G McCarthy, C O'Connor for Gardiner.

THE ACTION

THE GREATEST MUNSTER final of them all. A second provincial title in three years for the Déise and Waterford's first Munster final win over Cork since 1959.

Cork were five points up after six minutes as Garvan McCarthy's daisy-cutter slipped between Stephen Brenner's legs. Dan Shanahan snapped a puck-out above John Gardiner and drove over Waterford's opener. He scored 1-3 in that opening half to keep Justin McCarthy's men in contention. On the quarter hour mark, Eoin Kelly shrugged off Jerry O'Connor under the Old Stand and finished over Donal Óg Cusack from a tight angle.

Brian Corcoran's second of the afternoon made it a five-point game again. Shanahan replied instantly as he grabbed Eoin Kelly's delivery on the edge of the square and fired past Cusack. A mammoth Ken McGrath point from between his own '45' and '65' left three between them at the break (1-14 to 2-8).

John Mullane scored within seconds of the restart but then got his marching orders from referee Sean McMahon for an off the ball incident with Brian Murphy. He received a one-month suspension that saw him sit out the All-Ireland semi-final loss to Kilkenny.

Paul Flynn pointed immediately after the red card as the Ballygunner man took up the mantle. Waterford were two points down when Flynn stood over a 30-metre free. The dipper deceived Donal Óg Cusack and Diarmuid O'Sullivan on the line as the ball ended in the top corner of the Cork net (3-12 to 1-17).

With two minutes left, James Murray and Declan Prendergast denied Jerry O'Connor a certain Cork goal. Eoin Murphy cleared and Seamus Prendergast grabbed the ball and rifled over to give the 14 men a two point advantage, before Tom Kenny soloed up the other end and popped over a point.

★★★★★

"

I NEEDED TIME on my own before big games, just to get my head right.

I always went for a spin in the morning in my own in the car, just to get myself focused before we got on the bus. Even for 10 or 15 minutes... *out for a spin*. I always did that. Get out on my own and no one around me.

I went for a spin around Kilmeaden, for 10 or 15 minutes out the road. Just to get my focus ready on what was going to happen and then back in to meet the lads on the bus... and then we're going.

On the Saturday, I nearly always went for a walk in Tramore. I'd go for a walk on my own down around the sand dunes. The night before the 2002 Munster final, I did that. One of my friends got married on the Friday and all the lads were on the beer for the weekend! I remember going for a walk that Saturday night and sitting down on the rocks and to be honest, I nearly fell asleep!

I was so relaxed! It was a lovely evening.

I didn't like rushing. I always wanted to have everything ready and go down. I needed that before I met the boys on the bus. Myself and Tony Browne nearly always sat together.

We'd sit close enough to the back and have a bit of craic. We'd always have a laugh on the bus. We weren't too nervous. We couldn't wait for the game obviously but we'd have a laugh going up on the bus. You'd be looking at all the buses heading off and all the lads on the beer!

You'd see them all pulled in and we'd be going past them having a laugh. The bus journey was always nice and relaxed.

We used to go to the training college up in Thurles; that's where Justin McCarthy always brought us. We knew it was a big game when we were going in there. You had enough time. You had your routine. You had your sandwich, and your cup of tea. You might go for a stroll or you might hit a few balls.

Justin normally went through the team.

The college was very quiet; it was lovely, it was a very tranquil place. Justin loved going somewhere quiet before all the games... we loved it as well. You would hear the odd shout here and there, but you couldn't hear much. It was full of lovely trees and gardens as we used to go for a stroll.

We'd leave the gates then... and a police escort up. The Square was absolutely hopping that day. You're talking about a time when there were 60,000 at a Munster final. The place was absolutely heaving. The Square was mobbed and the atmosphere was electric. You could feel it.

You might see someone you know and you might give them a smile or a wave.

They started very well.

They were a lot more structured than us. They were playing very close to how the game is played now. One-twos... pop passes and moving.

They were a very good team. They had pace.

They got a flukey goal; it went through Stevie Brenner. At one stage, it was like they were going to tear away from us. Brian Corcoran got two brilliant points. I gave a bad pass; Tom Kenny went past me, I couldn't catch him and he tapped it over. They were flying and I remember saying to Tony that we need to slow it down.

If they got one more goal, we were in trouble.

We hung in there. Dan Shanahan was brilliant in the first-half... Dan was unreal. He got 1-3. He got a couple of scores off John Gardiner and settled us down. We got back into the game. We hung in at times in the first-half; we weren't playing great but we got goals when they were needed.

Eoin Kelly got an unbelievable goal. Dan got a great goal; caught it over Diarmuid O'Sullivan. Kelly ran down the sideline... a famous goal and a famous celebration. That kept us in the game, but they looked a better team in the first-half.

They had pace... Jerry O'Connor and Tom Kenny in midfield. There was no team giving the pop-pass back then, but they were doing that and getting the return ball and moving. It was hard to deal with at times.

I used to love covering at centre-back and covering behind the wing backs. but with Cork, you had to be careful because they would give the ball to the fella in front of you. Now, they would go long, they would mix it up. Nowadays you have a way of playing and that's it but Cork would mix it up. They were very hard to play against.

There were three or four times in that game where they went past us and were gone, and you couldn't catch them. I remember the noise from their crowd was unreal.

I had great battles with Niall McCarthy; it was the first time I marked him. He was a tough player, but he was honest. He was a traditional centre-forward, in the middle of everything; he gave everything for that Cork team. He wasn't going to get three or four points every game, but he was going to cause chaos.

I didn't mind marking him. I didn't mind marking a robust player, I didn't mind at all. I was used to being that myself at centre-forward anyway. That was the first of many battles we had for the next five or six years. I wouldn't have known him beforehand but I would have known him afterwards, because he came across as a lovely fella.

A real honest, tough fella that you'd love on your team. It wasn't his best game. In the first-half, I was only steady but I grew into the game as it went on. At times at centre-back you have to be steady, you can't be clearing five or six balls. That's what I felt in that first-half I had to do. They could have been out of sight.

I wasn't playing brilliant, I wasn't playing poor, but I needed to get going and get the team going. I felt that at times... *I have to get more on the ball.* Eoin Murphy gave me a decent hand-pass and I put it over the bar.

There was a bit of a breeze. We were playing into the town end and lads will tell you that it is the scoring goal in Thurles. You always feel for some reason that you can reach the goal. Back then, it was a long range point. Nowadays, they wouldn't even bat an eyelid at it! I put everything into that ball to reach it and it barely went over the bar. Nowadays, lads would sail that over with 20 or 30 yards to spare. It was a good score for me to get into the game.

I *loved* centre-back. I loved centre-forward, I always loved centre forward. I was there centre-forward or wing forward for Waterford for seven or eight years. Fergal Hartley was after retiring so maybe it was a natural switch for me. I was playing there for the club if things went wrong; especially underage I would have played a lot of hurling centre-back.

I missed the first half of the National League. I had a clean-out of my knee in January. I came back for the Limerick game in Walsh Park and I was wing back and played well. I was wing back up to the league final. They put me at centre-back against Clare and it was probably one of my best games for Waterford up in Thurles.

That was it then really, you weren't getting moved. I loved it; it was probably my favourite five or six years of my career back there.

We regrouped just before half-time. We were lucky enough we were only three points down considering Cork were after doing a lot of the hurling. We were hanging in there. We regrouped at half-time and agreed, 'Lads, look… this is our chance now, we haven't really hurled yet!'

We weren't great against Tipp either in the semi-final. Paul O'Brien got the goal to dig us out of it. We knew we had to hurl and we were fired up at half-time knowing that it was such a big game, a Munster final against Cork… *we hadn't hurled well, but we were still in the game.* Probably the same as the year before, when we out-hurled Cork in the first-half without getting the scores and they hung in there and saw it out.

Going out after half-time, we were fired up.

John Mullane got a great score just after half-time. A minute or two later, as he said himself, he saw red. He reacted. Back then, corner-backs were tough and tight, there would be niggles going on… he reacted to it and he was caught. At the time, I remember thinking… *We're under pressure!* If Cork get a run on you, they're very hard to stop.

Paul Flynn stood up and was great in that second-half. He got a couple of scores to keep us in the game. Every ball mattered after that. When you have Joe Deane, Brian Corcoran, Jerry O'Connor, Ben O'Connor… they take some watching and they could destroy you. Ronan Curran got a great score in the second-half: he caught a ball and ran up the pitch and it was like Cork were coming on top then.

Flynn's goal changed the whole outlook of the game.

I was back far enough. It was in him, because in the 2002 county final Mount Sion played Ballygunner and we played some great hurling, and at the end of the game we were only three points up after all the hurling we played… and he went for a dipper and he hit the crossbar from 30 yards. It was very close.

We saw him doing that in training so many times; just before training he was always trying dippers and trying things. He had some unbelievable skill. And he tried it.

I still say he was probably surprised it went in, because if you look at it I think Dan put off Diarmuid O'Sullivan and Donal Óg Cusack couldn't see what was happening on the line. Ger Canning said it… *Only Paul Flynn would try that!*

He had that skill and he could do stuff that a lot of normal lads couldn't do. That goal changed the game and it gave us the belief. We forgot we had 14 men then, I'll be honest. We didn't play the second-half like we had 14 men, which was a fair credit to the team.

I remember actually enjoying the game. *This is what you play for.* I really remember enjoying that match in the second-half… down to the wire against Cork up in Thurles.

Growing up, you'd be saying, 'Jesus are Waterford ever going to come back as a strong county and play in a Munster final?' It was a mini-All-Ireland back then really, if you think about it.

'Bull' Phelan got fouled over in front of the Old Stand, and I had a free.

There was a bit of play; it came back out and I struck it in again. I probably put it over where I should have put it. Ronan Curran put it right down the centre. It wouldn't happen now; they would have worked the ball out from that spot. He put it right back down where I was and I had no real option but to catch it because Diarmuid O'Sullivan was on me at that stage, and Ben O'Connor was just sitting behind me, and he would have put it over the bar and it would have been a draw.

For the hurling we did in the second-half, it would have been a disaster. It was a catch I felt I had to make. It wasn't my best catch; it was a good catch but it was probably one of my most important. It was a catch I would feel I should be making. Sully didn't really go for it properly, he went with a one-handed swing.

I would have been going mad if I didn't catch it. At that stage, we knew the game was up. There was only a minute of injury-time which shows how fast and how flowing that game was.

I was captain. It was a great buzz… the dressing-room was great.

We won our first Munster final in Páirc Uí Chaoimh but Thurles was always home for us. It was always the benchmark, how you played up in Thurles in Munster Championship… packed stadiums, Cork at their best, us at our best.

It was such a big game to win, we were over the moon. We walked in to Thurles; the traffic was crazy, we were meeting in the Anner Hotel. I had a pint with Tony in one of the pubs. Mullane was there as well, we had right craic.

Back then, you could walk in and meet all the lads. I met a few of my friends and family and had a pint; went up to the hotel then. I'll never forget that bus home and having the craic and that. That's what it's for. We go out and play the games and try the best we can, but the craic afterwards on that bus coming down on a lovely sunny evening… I'll never forget that.

We only won four Munster titles so they're priceless really.

I have the jersey. My wife Dawn got an All Star jersey framed for me from Singapore. I keep them. It will be nice for the kids, they don't even know I played the game! You have to keep something. I don't know where I'm going to put these things but they're somewhere at home. The jersey is actually massive!

Everyone wore huge jerseys back then. It's an iconic jersey, the jersey we wore that year. It's a lovely jersey. If you see it, it reminds you of that era straight away.

I know that the team did give everything and we got to a level that, when I started out, I didn't know if we would ever get to that level. That's the truth. We played in so many big games and we had such a roller-coaster of matches… and the crowds back then. A first round could be a sell-out.

They were massive, *massive games* and massive days out. We had enough chances to win an All-Ireland so there was obviously something missing that we didn't win it. We have no one to blame but ourselves.

You have to accept that and put up with that.

I played in eight All-Ireland semi-finals, and I only won one, so you have no one to blame but yourself. When I look back on it, I couldn't have done any more. If that's your lot, *that's your lot*… what can you do?

I know myself, I couldn't have done any more and all the lads would feel the same. I never went on a summer holiday, or a stag until I finished hurling with Waterford, all that type of stuff. It was never done. It never came into your mind.

You just trained from the first of January on, you enjoyed Christmas obviously… then you trained and you did everything you could to try and win an All-Ireland.

If it didn't happen, *it didn't happen.*

99

DAN SHANAHAN

WATERFORD 1-22 TIPPERARY 3-13
All-Ireland SHC Quarter-Final
Croke Park
JULY 23, 2006

Dan Shanahan shows his love for his county as he celebrates after scoring against Tipperary in the 2006 All-Ireland quarter-final victory in Croke Park in 2006.

★ **WATERFORD:** C Hennessy; D Prendergast, T Feeney, E Murphy; T Browne, K McGrath (0-1), B Phelan; S O'Sullivan, D Bennett (0-6); **D Shanahan (1-5)**, S Prendergast, E Kelly; J Mullane (0-3), M Walsh (0-1), E McGrath (0-3). Subs: J Murray for Phelan, J Kennedy for Bennett, P Flynn (0-3) for O'Sullivan, S Molumphy for S Prendergast, P O'Brien for E McGrath.

★ **TIPPERARY:** B Cummins; D Fanning, P Curran, P Ormonde; E Corcoran, C O'Mahony, H Moloney; P Kelly (0-1), S McGrath; J Carroll (2-0), F Devanney, J O'Brien (0-1); L Corbett (0-2), D Fitzgerald, E Kelly (1-8). Subs: W Ryan (0-1) for Devanney, S Butler for O'Brien, C Morrissey for McGrath, K Dunne for P Kelly.

THE ACTION

THE CROKE PARK hoodoo was laid to rest at long last.

Waterford lost three All-Ireland semi-finals (1998, '02 and '04) and an All-Ireland quarter-final ('05) in Dublin before they came out on top in a thriller with Tipperary.

The sun finally shone on the Déise in the capital. Man of the Match Dan Shanahan was on song from start to finish... and 1-5 from play sealed his second All Star award.

In the first minute, Big Dan plucked a high ball out of the air, took on the Tipp defence and banged it over the bar. Less than 60 seconds later, John Carroll crashed the ball to the Waterford net. That set the tone for an end-to-end encounter.

Eoin Kelly walloped a 20-metre free past six Waterford defenders to give Tipp a 2-5 to 0-8 lead. Shanahan added two more points to his total before he was fouled for an injury-time penalty. Brendan Cummins tipped over Ken McGrath's effort as Waterford went in a point up at the break (0-13 to 2-6).

Seven minutes into the second-half, the unstoppable Shanahan slipped inside Eamonn Corcoran and belted the ball past Cummins into the Hill 16 End. His 11th championship goal. Croke Park erupted.

Waterford got on a roll. Paul Flynn, Michael Walsh, and John Mullane all split the posts. Eoin Kelly and Brick bossed the midfield exchanges as Tipp replaced their pairing. The gap was seven points with five minutes of normal time left. Carroll blasted home his second goal to set up a grandstand finish. Shanahan replied with his fifth white flag of the afternoon. A free from Tipp's Eoin Kelly left just a goal in it entering injury-time.

Babs Keating's men bombarded the Waterford goal but Brick Walsh broke out of defence with ball in hand and victory was theirs at last at GAA HQ.

★★★★★

"

THAT DAY, THE confidence was up.

Anyone who knew me, knew I was a confidence player. When I got the first point, I *grew*. It was one of the best games I ever played in my life above in the biggest stage of them all in Croke Park.

I could have picked the Clare game in 2004 when it set me alight. That was my first big game. I picked this one just on my own performance; it was a great team performance as well. My own performance that day was exceptional, probably one of the best games I ever played and there's very little talk about it.

In some of the games I played against Cork, I wasn't consistent. I would have got two goals but yet I wouldn't have touched the ball that often.

The fact that we hadn't won in Croke Park since 1998 was a massive thing for us going into that game. There was always the question, 'Could Waterford win in Croke Park?' Tipp had beaten us in the championship that year above in Páirc Uí Chaoimh. Eoin Kelly got 2-9 that day. I scored a goal the same day but it just wasn't enough. Ken McGrath was injured and a few more of the lads.

We had a massive training camp in the Curragh and everything went well for us. We had a brilliant trip. We trained hard up there; we were up at six in the morning, training hard, carrying logs… that kind of stuff, physical activity, mental activity. I think it really set us up for the year ahead.

It didn't pay off in the early rounds of the championship, but I think it stood to us that day above in Croke Park; the connection we had together. We had leaders on the field.

We were also hurting going into that game. The likes of Ken McGrath, Brick and John Mullane didn't want to be beaten by Tipp again; didn't want to be known as a team that couldn't win in Croke Park. The Curragh experience really set us alight.

Ken was going across a pool and broke his toe! He broke it in Waterford but he aggravated it again so he missed a bit of the championship because of it.

Hugh Moloney was on me for a while and, when I got the goal, it was Eamonn Corcoran. He was switched over to try and stop me. The points I got that day were unbelievable and I just played so well... *we just played so well*. You don't go out to destroy a fella, you go out to do your best. I started well that day and Hugh was taken off me.

I can still remember the goal... the fact that Brendan Cummins was such a good goalkeeper. Eamonn Corcoran dived in to flick the ball away and I sold him with a sidestep just to come inside him. The minute I turned Corcoran, there was only one thing on my mind... *GOAL*. There wasn't anything fancy about it, it was on my left side; I deliberately came onto my left side so I could finish strong into the corner.

I knew Cummins, who was coming out to me, wouldn't stop me.

The trick for me that day was going in behind the goal to see the fans.

In 1998, it was the old Croke Park. In 2006, it was the new Croke Park. It was massive for us to win up there in the new Croke Park and to celebrate into the Hill 16 end with the Waterford supporters. I came across the goal and kissed the jersey coming out the other side. It was never a big-headed thing for me, it was just pure relief that I got a goal in Croke Park... that the work I put in had paid off.

After that, I just grew again. I got some fantastic scores from play and not being big-headed... but Tipp just couldn't handle me that day.

I studied opposing goalkeepers.

The first thing you do as a finisher in the game is try to go to his weak side to upset him. You see great goalkeepers that are hugely confident on their good side. I would have studied Donal Óg Cusack, I would have studied Brendan Cummins... even Davy Fitzgerald. He used to always crunch down and use his spring to make a save if it was above his shoulder.

I studied those goalkeepers. Brendan was a fantastic goalkeeper, but sometimes he had to twist his body to make a save; and I got a few goals against him after I studied him to see where I should put the ball.

That's something, even to this day in club hurling, that I still do.

If I go to the field, with no goalkeeper, I'd be trying to hit the stanchion or the post. With a goalkeeper then, you know if he's in there, that you can put it to that side. If you're used to hitting the post or that side of the goal, it will go in.

I spent a lot of time practicing these things... to finish the ball. I got 21 goals in my championship career, so I knew how to finish the ball.

With the new Croke Park, we were brought upstairs to have a beer afterwards. We were so not used to going up in a lift to have food or drinks. After winning, to go up into the corporate boxes and look out… having your sandwich or cup of tea or dinner, remembering what you have achieved! We didn't win an All-Ireland but it was a big win for us in Croke Park.

To see what you had achieved, to look out and think… *Wow, what a stadium, what a day we're after having today.*

It wasn't a big superstition but I used to always have the same gear. The same underwear, the same clothes I wore. I always wore two pairs of socks and they would have to be the same socks I wore the previous day. My mother used to have it all ready for me, to be honest with you, for championship day.

I'd always say a prayer before a match, to be brutally honest with you. I have no difficulty in admitting that. I said a prayer inside in the toilet about a half an hour before a match. I would have prayed, 'Please God, can I have a good day today?' If it worked out, it worked out. It did some days and it didn't other days.

My prayers weren't answered some days and some days they were. Against Tipperary that day, they were well answered.

Usually, I was last out on the field, or second last. Paul Flynn and myself were always last or second last. I just waited until everyone else was gone and, then, I went myself. They were just things I did. Everyone is different. I'd just let Flynners go ahead of me… and I'd be the last out to get that buzz and soak up the feeling.

I shouldn't have played against Offaly in the National League that year. I got a shot off Doctor Tom Higgins before the match and it didn't work out for me. I got a small bit of abuse from the stands above in Birr, I can remember that.

Things were going very bad for me. When they went bad for me, they went BAD! I got one or two jeers from the stands from the Waterford supporters… *Take him off… He's useless…* that kind of stuff. The only way you can answer that is by going out and playing well, and doing your best.

I had a bad day that day as in I shouldn't have played, that's the big regret. I should have said to the management, 'I'm not feeling well' but I did the macho thing and tried to get through it. I know now I should have said, 'I'm not able to play today!' That's what you did back then… get an injection to kill the pain and get through the game. It didn't work out for me that day.

The hardest thing for me was that my mam and dad and brothers would have been in the stands and they would have heard people say nasty things about me. My uncles would have been there as well. They never got up and gave out to anyone; they just took it on the chin and left it off until I had my good day.

You would hear them. When you're playing well, you don't hear these things. When you're not playing well, you hear these things. It does upset you, but what can you do about it?

You go away, you train hard; they're not the people below in the field in January or February, putting in the effort to try and play well in every game.

That's what you have to take when you're a sportsperson.

You're going to have bad days, you're going to get criticised whether it's in the newspapers or in the stands. You're going to have to take it on the chin, and go out and do your best the next day, and see can you right the wrong.

Gerry Fitzpatrick came on board in 2004 and he changed my appearance altogether. It was unbelievable. If you look at two pictures… the 2004 Munster final team picture and the '03 Munster final team picture, I must have been down two stone.

I wasn't getting my game in 2002 or '03 when Justin McCarthy came in, but I do know for a fact that Justin told Paddy Joe Ryan, 'This fella is going to come good!' He had trust in me. Justin trusted me and believed in me.

Gerry came in and he brought a different approach, mentality-wise, physicality-wise… his psychology. He'd just tell you, 'You're looking well,' and it would put a spring in your step. That's what players want to hear; that you're looking well, you're looking fit.

All of a sudden you're saying to yourself, 'Jesus Christ, Gerry notices I'm fit!' It was down to him. I can remember going to the Clonea Strand Hotel squatting 120kg, 140kg… 3x10 just to be up to the pace for the summer hurling. That was all down to Gerry and his gym programme, his psychology; understanding what you had to put your body through to get to that fitness to be an inter-county hurler.

I have to thank him for that. I have to thank Justin as well because he believed in me.

It doesn't bother me that I didn't win an All-Ireland medal for the simple reason that I can assure you, from the bottom of my heart, I gave everything I could to try and get up the steps in Croke Park. Knowing that I did everything, what I sacrificed in my life to try and win an All-Ireland... I spent 14 years there since 1996 when Tony Mansfield took me in.

I got dropped in 1997, but from '98 on I was a member of that panel or on the team. I gave it everything I could on and off the field. *Did I enjoy myself after winning a championship game?* You're damn right I did. That was all part of it.

You have to enjoy life and I did enjoy it; and we did enjoy it. I've no regrets. I gave everything I had to try and win the ultimate goal. I put it to you this way, Steven Gerrard never won a Premier League medal but it didn't make him a bad player. He won a Champions League medal. *Do you know what I'm saying?*

Just because Dan Shanahan, Ken McGrath or John Mullane didn't win an All-Ireland, that doesn't mean they're bad hurlers. We gave it everything we could at the time.

We met some serious teams in Kilkenny; we slipped up against some teams like Limerick in 2007. I think Kilkenny in 1998 was our best opportunity to win an All-Ireland. I watched the game recently, it popped up on my phone. The amount of ball we wasted that day was bad. I would never say it was a poor Kilkenny team or an average Kilkenny team.

The one thing I would change is that if I was marking JJ Delaney again, I would have got more aggressive. He always followed me. I would have got more aggressive, not dirty, but more aggressive... use my size. I was trying to hurl these fellas.

Maybe I should have used my hurling brain a bit more and try get aggressive under the high ball because JJ was outstanding under the high ball. I loved to catch ball when maybe I should have pulled, if you know what I'm saying. That's the only regret I have with playing Kilkenny, that I never used my size and my aggression a bit more.

I'm disappointed obviously not to win an All-Ireland, *hugely disappointed*, but that's sport and that's life. I can assure you I gave it everything I could to try and do that but it didn't happen. We met better players and better teams on the day.

"

SEAMUS PRENDERGAST

WATERFORD 0-20   KILKENNY 0-18
National Hurling League Final
Semple Stadium
APRIL 29, 2007

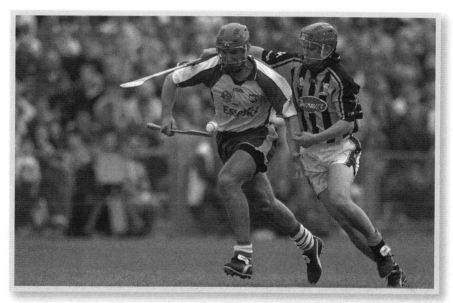

Seamus Prendergast shakes off the attention of Kilkenny's Tommy Walsh in Semple Stadium, as Waterford powered to the National League title in 2007.

★ **WATERFORD:** C Hennessy; E Murphy, D Prendergast, J Murray; T Browne, K McGrath (0-3), A Kearney; M Walsh, S Molumphy; E Kelly (0-8), **S Prendergast (0-3)**, S Walsh; J Mullane (0-2), D Shanahan (0-1), J Kennedy (0-1). Subs: P Flynn (0-1) for S Walsh, E McGrath (0-1) for Murray, S O'Sullivan for Kennedy.

★ **KILKENNY:** PJ Ryan; N Hickey, B Hogan, JJ Delaney; J Tyrrell, PJ Delaney, T Walsh; D Lyng (0-1), W O'Dwyer; E Brennan (0-1), M Comerford (0-2), R Power (0-2); H Shefflin (0-12), J Fitzpatrick, A Fogarty. Subs: E Larkin for Fitzpatrick, E McCormack for Fogarty.

THE ACTION

LATE POINTS FROM Eoin Kelly and Seamus Prendergast sealed Waterford's first league title since 1963. Michael Walsh lifted the cup in front of a sea of white and blue.

Aidan Kearney caught the eye at corner-back as he held All-Ireland final hero Aidan Fogarty scoreless and drove out with possession. Ken McGrath was Man of the Match, while Walsh also rose to the challenge at midfield. Seamus Prendergast stood as tall as the Round Tower in the closing stages with two crucial points, and three in all.

It was a tight and tense affair throughout. The sides were level on nine occasions during the opening 35 minutes. Three long-range frees from Ken McGrath handed the Déise a 0-11 to 0-9 half-time cushion. Henry Shefflin smashed a 20-metre free wide, and Waterford goalkeeper Clinton Hennessy raced off his line to flick the ball away from King Henry in injury-time.

The Cats claimed five points without reply at the start of the second period. Hennessy deflected a blistering shot from Eddie Brennan over the bar. It took Waterford 15 minutes to add to their tally through Eoin Kelly. Points from Eoin McGrath, Dan Shanahan and sub Paul Flynn levelled it at fifteen points all.

Martin Comerford and Richie Power edged the black and amber back in front but John Mullane got two late points to tie the game. Seamus Prendergast grabbed a Ken McGrath free and split the posts to give Waterford an 18-17 advantage.

Shefflin made it all square entering four minutes of injury-time with his 12th point of the day. Mullane won the next puck-out and fed the ball back to Kelly to lift and strike over the bar. His eighth white flag. Seamus Prendergast then gathered the sliotar from a throw-in and the Ardmore man sent over the insurance score. His third point from play on a productive afternoon.

★★★★★

66

ON THE SAME day, my sister Lisa won a camogie league medal with Waterford. My now wife Aisling was playing with her as well. My brother Declan and myself won the hurling league... and my sister and wife won the camogie one.

It was on a little bit earlier, in Portlaoise, but they got back for some of the hurling match. I wasn't going out with Aisling at the time. After every game, I met my family out on the field. My father, my mother, my uncle and my other brother Patrick were up at every match. They always came out on the pitch... win, lose or draw. I remember meeting them and they were delighted, jumping around the place!

There was a decent enough crowd, though it wasn't a full house or anything like that.

It was a long time since we beat Kilkenny in a match like that. We won after a tight battle against probably the best team of the noughties. They never went out to lose a game so it was a big win for us. Tony Coffey was dancing in the stand when I saw the replay of it!

I got three points myself that day; two near the end. One of them was from a throw-in. Eoin McGrath went for the clash and it broke out to me, and I turned around and I had a bit of space... and tapped it over the bar.

We had it tough every way with the Kilkenny defenders. They were able to hurl and they were able to dish it out as well! I never got any words from a Kilkenny fella, they only hurled! They didn't need to chat.

There were other fellas that mightn't be as good that would spout away, but I never took much notice of it, to be honest with you.

That was the year we went on to win the Munster final against Limerick, and then they beat us in Croke Park. We had two games with Cork before Limerick beat us in the semi-final.

It was one of our better years and when you look back, it was the year we could have won an All-Ireland, if we got over Limerick.

It was one of our best chances. In 2004 as well, we got caught in the All-Ireland semi-final as well with Kilkenny. There were three teams at that stage... Cork, ourselves and Kilkenny, and there was nothing between us.

I always got on well with Justin McCarthy. I spent a good bit of time above in his ball-alley. It was in Passage West, just beside his house. He took a few of us one-on-one to get our hurling skills up to scratch. Myself and Declan went up there, Eoin Murphy was up there, Brick was up there, James Murray... a good few went up to help our first-touch and that. He was very good to us. We were definitely up a dozen times or more.

In the house he showed us his medals and his trophies, and gave us a bowl of soup and whatever afterwards. He was good to us, in fairness.

It was to speed up everything. We were coming in at the time from junior hurling in the earlier days with Justin and he wanted to get us to a higher level. He saw that there was plenty of potential. We went up in December or January time, before the season started, to get tuned up.

Another couple of times throughout the year he'd invite us up. If we had a spare evening, we'd call up.

He touched up our hurleys. He would pare it down a little bit. If he thought it was too heavy, he would take a little bit off it. He was a perfectionist with the hurleys. He lightened mine a little bit to speed up the swing of it; he thought I had a heavy hurley.

You could get four or five hurleys off a hurley maker and there could be three real nice ones. He'd look at them. He'd see a new one and he'd say, 'I'll touch that one up'.

There was always two of us going together. Myself and Declan. We could have a chat about training and how things were going... going well or going bad. You always had somebody to talk to about the training.

We spent a good bit of time marking each other too! If Declan was full-back and I was full-forward or whatever. We marked each other a good bit in training. Brothers went out the window then! When you're playing for the county, you have to go at full tilt. Whoever is marking you, you have to go hard at it.

That was the same with all the players. I got as many hard belts at training as I did in a championship match; there was plenty of fellas that would let you know they were around.

When I started, football was the main thing in Ardmore back in 2000. Now, all the young lads only want to play hurling. Football is after taking a backseat.

A lot more people went to the matches because of us. That brought on the club; they all wanted to be involved when we were doing well with the county team. More people got involved with the club.

I remember when we won the first Munster final in 2002, I was only starting out. The whole team went over to the terrace and I could pick out 20 people from Ardmore! Young and old. It was great. There were people who wouldn't normally go to matches that were there and enjoying it. The run we had when I was playing; people got great excitement out of it and they got great travel.

A lot of young lads, whom I'm playing with now, travelled to all of those games with their fathers when they were youngsters. It helped with their love of the game definitely.

I was lucky enough at under-14, I was picked for the Tony Forristal. I was playing away up through the ages to minor and under-21. That helped. I played with the Waterford intermediate team when I was 19… the second team. I did okay in that game and a few months later, Gerald McCarthy rang me up and asked me to come for trials and that's when I realised that if I put the effort into this, I might make it.

The first year I came on as a sub in championship and after that, I started most games. Hard work and commitment is a big part of inter-county. If you can give that, you have a good chance.

I relaxed the night before a big match. I used to go to Mass most Sundays, a good few of us used to do that. Even when we were away with Justin, we'd go to Mass. Ten or 12 of us would head down with him.

I don't know if it helped, but we used to do it anyway! As the year went on, more fellas would go!

I had only one disappointment, that I didn't win an All-Ireland. Other than that, I enjoyed it. I love playing hurling. I enjoyed playing for Waterford. The commitment and the time is not a consideration when you enjoy it. And I made great friends.

Hurling has helped me in my career. I'm Territory Manager with Norbrook and after playing with Waterford, people know you straight away. I cover the south-east where all the hurling is played! It's a start. You have to work hard afterwards to keep the job.

I did enjoy it. I won my All-Ireland with the club which was a highlight of my career; it was where I started and to climb the Hogan Stand steps with my family and the friends I played with all my life was an unbelievable feeling.

I can't complain too much!

99

CLINTON HENNESSY

WATERFORD 3-17   LIMERICK 1-14
Munster SHC Final
Semple Stadium
JULY 8, 2007

Despite spending eight years in Boston, Clinton Hennessy (above, clearing the ball against Limerick in the Munster final victory in 2007) came home and won the No 1 jersey in the Waterford camp.

★ **WATERFORD: C Hennessy**; E Murphy, D Prendergast, A Kearney; T Browne, K McGrath (0-1), J Kennedy; K Moran, M Walsh; D Shanahan (3-3), E Kelly (0-4), S Molumphy (0-2); J Mullane (0-3), S Prendergast (0-1), P Flynn (0-2). Subs: J Murray for Moran, E McGrath (0-1) for Kennedy

★ **LIMERICK**: B Murray; M O'Riordan, S Lucey, S Hickey; P Lawlor, B Geary, M Foley; D O'Grady (0-1), M O'Brien (0-1); M Fitzgerald (0-3), O Moran (0-1), N Moran; A O'Shaughnessy (0-3), B Begley (1-2), B Foley. Subs: K Tobin (0-2) for N Moran, P Tobin (0-1) for B Foley, P O'Dwyer for O'Brien.

THE ACTION

THE SUMMER OF Dan the Man. The Lismore forward was the hat-trick hero on Munster final day, scoring 3-3 on his way to winning Hurler of the Year.

The unstoppable Shanahan completed the championship with an outrageous 8-12 from play. He netted 21 championship goals between 2004 and '10.

There was only a point in it on the hour mark before Waterford blitzed their opponents 2-4 to 0-2 down the stretch. Two goals from Big Dan, and points from Eoin Kelly, Ken McGrath, Eoin McGrath and Paul Flynn.

Umbrella by Rihanna was No 1 in the charts. And wet gear was required on a rainy Sunday afternoon in Semple Stadium.

The Shannonsiders squandered two glorious goal-chances inside two minutes. The sliotar slipped out of Barry Foley's hands before Clinton Hennessy saved with his feet from Brian Begley. The Limerick goal eventually arrived in the seventh minute when Begley flicked a Brian Geary free to the net. Hennessy and his defenders argued that the big full-forward was in the square.

Limerick were a point up, 1-9 to 0-11, before Shanahan pounced on 51 minutes. The hard working Stephen Molumphy supplied Paul Flynn, who saw his shot brilliantly saved by Brian Murray before the No 11 swept home the rebound. John Mullane, scorer of three points, then carried a dog off the field.

Shanahan struck again with seven minutes to go when Michael Walsh picked him out. The third goal was a dream scenario for Dan. Seamus Prendergast sent in the ball and he was completely unmarked in front of the Killinan goal. Only Brian Murray to beat. 'There was no one within 20 yards of me. To be honest with you, I went for a crowd pleaser! When you're one-on-one with the goalkeeper and you're six points up, I knew that I could really rattle this one.'

Limerick got their revenge in the All-Ireland semi-final.

★ ★ ★ ★ ★

66

I REMEMBER THAT day, Brick Walsh gave me a small medal from an old woman.

A woman gave him a medal to give to the goalkeeper for some reason! A holy medal. I remember sticking it in my sock. When someone gives you something like that, I didn't want to just throw it in the bag. It was only a small holy medal and I stuck it inside my sock that day.

She gave Brick one as well.

It was a greasy day. There was a bit of rain at the start of the game and it rained at the end of the game too. The ball went down the line and Declan Prendergast slipped and Brian Begley cut in. He probably shouldn't have given me a chance from there really. It was at me and the only thing I could get on it was my foot.

I had my hurley ready to go, thinking he was going across the goals. He hit it straight at me and I stopped it with my foot.

Eoin Kelly from Tipp was the forward I feared most.

There's no doubt in my mind and I'll never probably change it! Because of his goal-scoring ability and the shot he had. How fast he could get a shot off. Kelly was lethal. The wrists he had; he could have the ball past you before you knew it. When he hit it… HE HIT IT!

For me, personally, winning a first Munster medal was great. It probably was a flattering scoreline with the goals we got late on. But it was nice to enjoy the last few minutes of it, knowing we had it won. We had a decent lead going into the last couple of minutes. Usually, you're hanging on in a big match and waiting for the whistle but in that one, we were in control.

We were going well that year; we won the league, confidence was high. We were at the peak of our powers.

I had the gear ready the night before. Just to make sure I had everything, and I even brought stuff that I didn't need. I didn't leave anything to chance with gear and studs and stud tighteners… I had everything, like! If lads were looking for something, I usually had it. Tape or grips, all that kind of stuff.

I'd replace the grips if there was a big match coming up, or every second match at least; put the fresh grips on them. A lot of it is in your head but you just try to be as prepared as you can be before you go out there.

I always had six of my own hurleys with me, because of penalties and 21-yard frees. You'd have four players in there with you. I always knew who was coming in with me. That was always picked beforehand, because sometimes that can cause confusion.

You'd have picked who was coming in for the penalty, and who was coming in for the '21'. That was all done beforehand. I had hurleys for all of them, if they wanted one.

I didn't get a lot of instructions. Short puck-outs weren't really a thing. Cork were doing it, but I was pucking to the likes of Dan Shanahan and Seamus Prendergast. *What's the point going short when you have lads like that who can win ball.* We were direct with Justin. There wasn't as much tactics as there would have been under Davy.

I was in Boston for almost eight years.

There was a fella from Ardmore over the hurling, Mike McGrath. He had said it to me when I was home one summer. I said I might be interested. When it got closer, at Christmas, I said, 'No, I won't!' I got a notion one day that I'd go for the summer and go for six months. I rang him and he said that the deadline for home-based players was April 10… and I said I'd go and I was gone within a week!

If I didn't do it that way, I would never have done it. While I was thinking about it, I was finding reasons *not* to go.

I loved it over there. At that stage, with the knockout championship here, you were playing with great players. The standard over there was really high. I played for Tipperary. The first year I was there, I played with PJ Delaney from Kilkenny, Colm Bonnar from Tipperary, Fergal McCormack from Cork and Ollie Moran from Limerick. Paul Shelly from Tipp was there another year, Conor Gleeson from Tipp and Mark Foley from Limerick. Limerick and Tipp were the big connections over there with the team I was playing for.

When I came back from Boston in 2003, Ardmore were up senior for the first time ever. We got a really tough start to senior. We had Mount Sion in our first game and we had Tallow, and then we had Lismore. We beat Lismore; I made two or three saves from Dan and I had a good game. I had another good game against Ballygunner… I was going well at that stage.

Waterford were going up to Antrim and Stevie Brenner had a back injury. It was after the Munster final of 2004 and Justin rang me to see would I be able to go up to Antrim. Stevie was injured and at that stage it was between Ian 'Iggy' O'Regan and Stevie for who would have been playing in the semi-final.

I went up to Antrim that weekend and there were two games, an A and a B game. I played in the second game, so that was my first game for Waterford. It's funny. My first game was here, where I'm living now, in Loughgiel!

I was going out with Michelle at the time and it was in her local pitch! Loughgiel Shamrocks. That's where I am now. Strange the way it pans out.

Before the 2005 All-Ireland quarter-final against Cork, I was probably playing the best hurling I ever played. In training matches, I was going well. We went up to Dublin the week before the quarter-final. It was a game amongst ourselves, an A vs B game in Parnell Park. I played really well, one of those good days.

We stayed out in Castleknock. Eoin Murphy said, 'You didn't do yourself any harm today!' I knew I was going well, but I wasn't sure.

I thought Justin mightn't do it because of what happened with Iggy the year before. He was brought in for the All-Ireland semi-final against Kilkenny. I still appreciate now Justin doing it because it was a brave thing to do. No matter how well I was going, it was a brave thing to do.

We played Clare in the qualifiers and they got four goals in Ennis and that opened the door. That weekend we were up in Parnell Park, he brought us to Croke Park for a walkaround. That wouldn't have been a normal thing. I couldn't get over the size of it.

Obviously, I had been in Croke Park watching matches but, down on the field, the whole place looked massive and daunting. I was looking at the crossbars in the goals and I thought they were high and stuff like that.

On the Tuesday night, Justin said, 'You might be playing on Sunday'. It was Thursday before he rang me to say that I was playing, but not to tell anybody. The team was announced on the Friday. One thing he did tell me was not to be saying much and not to be surrounding myself with people I didn't want to be around.

I was that way anyway coming up to a match. I'd lock myself away for a few days, stay out of somewhere I didn't have to be. I didn't bother going into the shopping centre in Dungarvan the Friday or Saturday before a match! It's just easier.

Things went well for me. I didn't do anything spectacular in that debut. I just did the simple things; my handling was good. It was just the fact I was new. I was trying to get through it without any major errors. You don't need to have a blinder; it was just about getting through it. That was a big game too.

From a selfish point of view, I saw it as a start. We lost the game but I got through it and I knew I was after grabbing hold of the position. It was up to me after that to improve and get better.

My family went to all the games. My mother and father, my sister and my brother, we had a lot of support in Ardmore, and first cousins were always there. Ardmore were good to support us, when the three of us were there... Seamus and Declan Prendergast and myself, there was always a good buzz around the village. Having three people from Ardmore on the team was huge.

When I made my debut that day in Croke Park, I had friends who flew home from Boston and from London. Sometimes, when you're in the middle of it, you don't really appreciate everything. You're focused on hurling and that's it.

I loved playing senior championship for Ardmore. We were never going to win a championship but just playing prime-time on a Sunday against the big clubs! We were competitive.

In my opinion, Seamus Prendergast was the best club hurler in Waterford for a good number of years. He was unbelievable for Ardmore, and Declan at the back.

It gave the village a buzz having the three of us on the Waterford team. There was always a bit of excitement if there was a big match coming up. It did a lot for people. You talk to people now and they still say they were great times.

EOIN MURPHY
(& EOIN KELLY)

WATERFORD 1-20 TIPPERARY 1-18
All-Ireland SHC Semi-Final
Croke Park
AUGUST 17, 2008

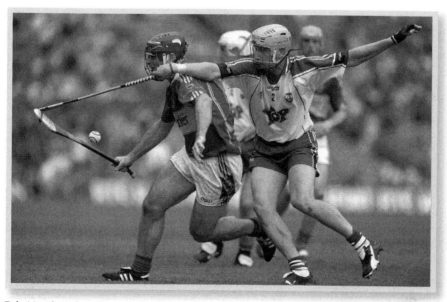

Eoin Murphy takes charge in the historic All-Ireland semi-final win over Tipperary in 2008.

★ **WATERFORD:** C Hennessy; **E Murphy**, K McGrath, D Prendergast; A Kearney, T Browne, K Moran; M Walsh (0-2), J Nagle; D Shanahan, S Prendergast, S Molumphy (0-2); E McGrath (0-2), **E Kelly (1-10)**, J Mullane (0-3). Subs: J Kennedy (0-1) for S Prendergast, P Flynn for Mullane, G Hurney for Nagle, S O'Sullivan for Shanahan.

★ **TIPPERARY:** B Cummins; E Buckley, P Curran, C O'Brien; E Corcoran, C O'Mahony (0-1), S. Maher (0-1); J Woodlock, S McGrath (0-3); S Callanan (1-2), H Moloney, J O'Brien; E Kelly (0-8), S Butler, L Corbett (0-1). Subs: P Stapleton for Corcoran (blood sub), M Webster for Butler, B Dunne (0-1) for O'Brien, P Kerwick (0-1) for Maloney, P Bourke for Woodlock.

THE ACTION

DAVY FITZGERALD AND John Mullane rolled around on the Croke Park turf after Waterford reached their first All-Ireland final in 45 years.

A summer that started with a nine-point loss to Clare under Justin McCarthy ended with an All-Ireland final against Kilkenny under the new manager. Davy Fitz only took over in June after a player vote went against McCarthy. The Clare man guided them back to Croker with backdoor victories over Antrim, Offaly and Wexford.

There was an explosion of emotion around the stadium as Waterford ended their semi-final heartbreak. They lost five prior to this (1998, '02, '04, '06 and '07).

Full-forward Eoin Kelly was one of the stars of the summer and was named Man of the Match after shooting 1-10. He scored 7-43 in that championship. The Passage man was subsequently nominated for Hurler of the Year and received his second All Star.

Tipperary went into the game as league and Munster champions, but Waterford raced into a six-nil lead after just nine minutes. The pace of corner-forwards Eoin McGrath and John Mullane was too hot for the Tipp backs. Eoin Kelly fired over five first-half points. Tipp's Eoin Kelly levelled the match at the break with his sixth of the afternoon (10 points each).

Waterford's Eoin Kelly bundled the ball past Brendan Cummins at the second attempt to give the underdogs a two-point lead on 56 minutes (1-15 to 0-16). Tipp went straight up the other end, however. as Seamus Callanan capitalised on uncertainty in the Déise defence and goaled in front of Hill 16. Pat Kerwick added a point for the Premier.

Waterford rose to the challenge with four unanswered points from Michael Walsh, sub Jack Kennedy and two Kelly frees. Liam Sheedy's men had the sliotar in the net in the last minute but referee Diarmuid Kirwan disallowed it for a square ball.

★ ★ ★ ★ ★

" "

I'LL NEVER FORGET the train journey home.

If we could have stayed on that train for 24 hours, we would have been happy. We had two carriages. My mam and dad, my sister and Leona, my wife, were down the carriages.

Davy allowed us to have a few drinks. We were trying to come to grips with… *Jesus, we've finally made it to a final, we get to experience the build-up to a final.* It was a case of enjoying the night but knowing what was coming around the corner as well. It was brilliant to be in the middle of our supporters on the train. Even walking down to say hello to my parents, I got nothing but cheers and 'well done' which is always nice. We didn't get to interact a huge amount with supporters. At that stage, they weren't allowed onto the field or anything.

Initially, we got to celebrate and had that experience in the dressing-room and that buzz. Davy brought us down to earth but he also knew that it was a huge hurdle for us to get over after being there so many times and not making it. We had all that built up. If we were to get on a bus and be on our own heading back home or had something to eat and jumped on a bus… it was lovely to have the train, I have to say.

It was a relief, not just for the players, but for the county and for all GAA people in Waterford to finally say… *the next three weeks is the build-up now.* That was a fantastic night when I think back; to be leaving Croke Park after playing a semi-final, having won and getting ready for a final.

The celebrations were unbelievable, I'll never forget it. Having played in five semi-finals at that stage, to finally get over the line, it was an unbelievable release.

2007 was a downer… Limerick! We had a brilliant year up to the semi-final after getting over Cork in a replay. Limerick then pipped us. We were coming to a stage where we thought our chance was gone. Thankfully, we got on the right side of the result in a semi-final for once.

My first touch was a drop shot out the field! Tony Browne hit a ball back to me. I always wanted to try it, having seen it before.

Here we go!

It was a nice place to find myself in.

I played most of my career with good awareness. That would have been one of my strengths, an awareness of who's around me or what's coming. Keeping things simple was always my motto. Pass the ball off. I wasn't blessed with being a brilliant striker of the ball.

The ball was going over towards the sideline, but I knew something was coming. I do remember in the moment that someone was coming and not from Waterford! A Tipperary player was coming... Lar Corbett.

I knew I was near the sideline as well. In my own head I said... *I'll get possession of the ball anyway.* I roll-lifted it and I thought... *I'll see what's going to happen here...* and then I could sense that they were coming at speed. I was conscious that I was going to be able to avoid it. He did clip me, but it wasn't very bad. For the most part, I did avoid it. He did go at full-tilt and he did want to blow me out over the line with a shoulder, but at that speed it's very hard to nail a shoulder.

I do remember that and I thought... *I'll see what will happen here!*

I was play-acting a little bit! I made a bit of a meal of it! I've been given a lot of stick since about taking a second before I went down to see... *Okay, I will go down here!* But it wasn't very bad. He did catch me on the helmet, there was a little nick from one of the bars and there might have been a little bit of blood.

The ref and the linesman were probably coming over to see is this fairly bad. He probably had enough momentum built up to do a bit of damage, especially on the head. I was cut alright but it wasn't as bad as I made it out to be! People still send it onto me in a WhatsApp group.

It's still on YouTube unfortunately! It comes under Big Hits in GAA! I'd say there were bigger ones!

I was marking Eoin Kelly that day.

He was a great, wristy player. He had great strength, especially in his legs and his lower half. He was fast, but I was probably able to match him in that department. He was just able to turn and twist. His skill level was really high and, of course, he had a great eye for a score and a goal in particular. I would have thought... *Keep the ball out of his hand as much as possible.* I took chances out in front of him, which was my game.

I think it was in that match where he tried to throw a dummy right and hit left, and I knew exactly what he was going to do and I got a good block. I blocked it down, got possession, hand-passed it to Ken… and Ken cleared it up. I felt really good and even that first touch of the ball, where I let fly on this thing and it came out the sweet spot of the hurley and I was like… *This is where I want to be.*

I was bang in the game then. Those little memories do come back to me now.

It was an up and down year.

Justin McCarthy left and then Davy Fitzgerald came in. There was a point to prove from earlier in the year; there was an added impetus for us. We carried that a little bit, even though Davy wouldn't have brought that up. It would have been within the group anyway, after what we did.

From the minute he came in, it was the intensity in training, the intensity in the drills. He had his style of play that he would have used in Third Level and other teams he would have worked with. He had that system with half-forwards working back and creating the space for the inside line.

It was an unbelievably professional set-up.

He brought in so many people; he got our gear washed, that kind of stuff. This was really bringing it to another level for us, which we hadn't experienced before; to arrive to training and have your gear hanging up, to walk into a dressing-room just with your hurley. Your gear is there, your boots are there, your bag is there… maybe he was trying to make us feel like we were professional.

This is what we think of you, this is what you deserve. Our self-worth and our self-value, maybe he was working on that.

I would have been very open to whoever came in. He did a lot in his playing career, he had seen a lot, he did a lot at Third Level and was successful with LIT. There was a little doubt around him having played against some of the people he was now coming in to manage. He wouldn't have maybe been the nicest on the field either; he had a cut and I'm sure people had a cut at him, it was a two-way thing.

I would have thought about it myself… *What is he going to be like as a people-manager and a team manager for inter-county.* But I think we needed something new and fresh. The majority just bought in and moved on. Training was hard. It was intense, it was very professional; things were laid out, new drills, new systems.

And the idea that you have to prove yourself again, that's never a bad thing. I would have played most of Justin's games; we got on really well and he would have backed me. There were games where I didn't play great and he backed me and supported me. There was a lot of loyalty there. Now, I had to prove it to someone else.

We had a very respectful relationship.

I came from very quiet surroundings. My own character wouldn't have been hugely confident coming from where I came from in Shamrocks. I was lucky to get to St Colman's in Fermoy and UCC, and start to buy into the thinking that I was good enough to play for Waterford, that I wasn't in a dreamworld.

I just adored Tony Browne and Fergal Hartley, and I went to see them playing under-21 in those finals with Offaly. I played on the Tony Forristal B team. I started to believe in myself, I started to apply myself and I really embraced the opportunities that came my way. I don't like confrontation, I'm not good at it. I much prefer being in harmony and having respect and knowing right and wrong as well. That would have been there with Davy. I had very little history with him from a playing standpoint so that respect would have been there.

I was lucky to come along in 2002, and in my first year starting I won a Munster medal. There's not a load of them floating around Waterford. When I look back, that was a great chance for us to win an All-Ireland. While we celebrated winning the Munster after 39 years, we still managed to get up to Croke Park in a good place playing Clare, got off to a good start and hit the ground running. We were on the crest of a wave and we managed to transition well enough to the semi-final and, I think, if we got over that, we could have won the All-Ireland by being on a wave. I thought that was a good opportunity.

In 2007, people talk about tiredness and having to play Cork the week before, playing three weeks in-a-row, but I don't buy into it. Limerick caught us with their goals; scoring five goals it was always going to be hard to come back from that. Maybe a little bit of complacency, and having beaten them already obviously gave them great motivation and impetus.

We were experienced enough that we should have been able to deal with that and be ready but we weren't, and they pipped us. It was a brilliant opportunity for us.

The All Star in 2006 was unbelievable.

Look, the sport is not really about individual awards. We had people from the club who represented the county and still do, and there's unbelievable talent but we are small. For me to get that award, it was a very proud moment for me. I try not to get too carried away with these things but the club, my family and the people who texted and who wrote and who came to celebrate...

We had an unbelievable night in Knockanore.

We had people in the house first and then we went up to Knockanore. There's a pub... The Shamrock Inn, it's gone now, and they led me in there with a piper. You couldn't make it up! They had piper out from Youghal with his kilt. It was surreal like!

That was just raw. I'll never forget the piper and I didn't know the piper was going to be there! I was like... *Oh my God!* When you're near the pipes and when they get going, when you hear them, they're very raw... and they go in and out through you. I wasn't far away from it all the way in and it's a really nice sound that lone piper.

We had an unbelievable night up there of celebration and joy. I hope that it inspired lads in the club onwards and let them see what can be achieved. Our family wouldn't be steeped in the GAA, though they would have played with the club and all that. They still love it, it's in their soul, it's in their core.

I still have the All Star in my house here, it's a lovely piece and it will always be there. I was lucky that year but the more I think about it, I always say I'm lucky and maybe it's an Irish thing... lucky I was *here*, lucky I was *there*... but maybe you can't be lucky all the time. Maybe I just need to stand back and say, 'I deserved it that year!'

EOIN KELLY

Eoin Kelly celebrates as Waterford make it through to the All-Ireland final after defeating Tipperary in 2008.

"

I REMEMBER GOING up to a lot of All-Ireland semi-finals, where I was thinking... *Are we going to win today?*

For some reason I *knew* we were going to win that game.

It was the relief of making a final. That team had been so close for so many years; players there for 10 or 15 years, never getting to a final... just to get to the final was a massive achievement for the team.

I had a hand injury at the start of the year and I was 50-50 for the Clare game. I decided myself that I wasn't ready to play so I missed the Clare game. That was Justin's last game and then I came back for Antrim. We played Antrim in Walsh Park and then we had Offaly and Wexford.

We got on a nice roll. Davy had me playing inside... I had a lot of room, myself and Mullane were the only two options in there, everyone else was pulled out. I got a load of good ball as well.

Everything fell right for me. I put in a good effort with Jimmy Payne. I had to get fit after the injury and Davy put me into Jimmy Payne, just the two of us, and Jimmy did wonders with me. The harder you train, the better you get.

I put in a serious effort and I got into the last three for Hurler of the Year, so something must have gone right.

In the gym, I did a bit of boxing, a bit of everything. We'd go down to Cheekpoint and there's a wicked hill in Cheekpoint; we used to run up that. He timed us doing a loop of Cheekpoint as well. There was a bit of everything in it. It stood to me.

With the games coming thick and fast, there was no celebrating after matches so we were four or five weeks concentrating on hurling, there was no side attractions. When we beat Tipp, the team didn't expect what we were facing into. We came home on the train and there were people carrying us off the train and everything.

What's going on here, like?

For the four or five weeks leading into the final, it got worse and worse. That's what happened to a lot of lads in the final, they just didn't turn up.

The players got rid of Justin.

If we didn't do something … *well our decision wasn't justified.*

'They got rid of the manager, it's not the manager that's the problem… it's the players that are the problem.' That was added pressure on us.

Going into that Tipp game, like no semi-final before, I said, 'We're definitely going to win today!' I knew in my head we were going to win. Tipp were league and Munster champions in 2008. They were raging hot favourites going into it. *I have a funny feeling we're going to win this today.*

Look, we got over the line in the end. We probably could have made it a small bit more comfortable. I'd say they had one eye on the final, being honest with you. It's very hard when that happens.

Dan kind of pulled on the ball with one hand.

I had Paul Curran, so I thought… *I have him on the right side now.*

I actually pulled on it perfect and it hit Brendan Cummins. The two of them got in each other's way then and the three of us were on the ground. I got my hurley to it and flicked it into the goal.

Here we go. We have it.

Then, they went straight up the field and got a goal.

Holy God. What are we doing?

There were some brilliant displays that day. Murph was brilliant, Clinton was very good in the goal, everyone played well… Ken, Tony… Mullane was brilliant.

Eoin McGrath had a great game. Jamie Nagle at midfield with Brick… everything clicked for us. There were other days, when we went up to semi-finals, only two or three fellas played really well. On this day, we had seven or eight that played really well. You're not going to get everyone playing well, but you need seven or eight fellas having good games.

That got us over the line in the end. Kevin Moran at wing back had a brilliant game as well. The relief of getting to the final was the main thing; so many years of knocking on the door, *knocking on the door*… Clare in 2002, we threw that one away; Kilkenny beat us in 2004, Wexford knocked them out of Leinster.

That never happened before. We were primed to meet them in the final if they won Leinster. No, we had to meet them in the semi-final and they got three fast goals and that was the end of that. In 2007… another disaster. This was weighing on fellas' minds.

We have to get over the line here at some stage.

Are we going to be the best team never to play in an All-Ireland final? It was just great to get there and say you played in an All-Ireland final.

My son Sean came on the field after the game. The partners of the lads, they all came out on the field. He just picked up the hurley and started walking off with it! I still have the pictures.

A horrible thing happened after that.

Jim Dee, the Lord have mercy on him, came to me after training between the semi-final and the final. 'There's a letter after coming for you.' It was giving out about the child being on the pitch… you should be ashamed of yourself having a child out of wedlock and the whole lot.

We had an open session then in Walsh Park and the drug testing fellas were

down and for the fifth week in-a-row, I got pulled again. Jim Dee came in...
'There's another letter after coming for you'. *It couldn't be as bad as the last one...*
but it was. The same kind of letter only it came from Kilkenny. I don't know what
their problem was.

I went bald-headed. I went out to see who gave the letter to Jim.

Your man, the drug tester said, 'You can't leave!'

'Out of my way,' I said.

They had to stay with you, the doping fellas, they had to stay by your side until
you did the business. 'I'm going to sort out this.'

'You can't leave.'

'Watch me,' I said. 'I'm going!'

He followed me out. 'Jim... who gave you the letter?'

'Don't tell me it was another bad letter?'

'Yeah!'

I don't know what it was aimed at; I don't know what people were trying to
achieve, were they trying to put me off playing a final?

A kid to be on the pitch with a father after winning an All-Ireland semi-final
and then to be abused about it. I thought it was a bit much.

I never got to the bottom of it. I don't know who took the letters off me and
said they'd deal with it. There was nothing ever done about it. You'd be talking
about online abuse the players are getting now.

One of them definitely came from Kilkenny, and I don't know where the other
one came from. It always leaves a sour taste in my mouth thinking of the All-
Ireland final because I always think about those letters. It left me with a sour
taste about the whole lot of it. I think the open session was 10 days before the
All-Ireland.

We'd one in Walsh Park on the Tuesday, and we'd one in Dungarvan on the
Thursday. It was disgusting.

Someone sent that photo to me framed. I have it up in the living room... that
picture. The *Irish Independent* had it. There was a write-up on the match and that
was the picture.

I got on great with Davy.

A change is better than a break. I got on really well with Justin, Justin was a gentleman. Davy came in with different ideas, some of the lads probably didn't like the ideas whereas I was on the side where his ideas were playing into my hands. I was the centre-point of the attack, everything was to be fed to me.

I was enjoying my hurling. I'd say if you asked Dan, he would say the opposite. Dan's thing in 2007 was drifting in, getting balls and scoring goals. Davy wanted Dan out the pitch. It suited some players, it didn't suit other players. I got on really well with him.

A funny thing about that year.

A couple of the lads backed me as first goal-scorer against Offaly, to score a goal at any time against Wexford, to get the first goal against Antrim and to score the first goal against Tipp. They were shouting down at me, 'Come on will ya… and get the goal! We're all waiting to win a few bob!'

I got the goal and that's why I turned and celebrated out that way.

They were just to the right-hand side where I ran off to… two or three of them there. This went on all year. There were fellas winning a fortune on me for first goal-scorer and to goal at any time. They did the same for the final, to get a goal at any time so they literally won money on every match.

I'd say the only fella that didn't back it was myself!

Do I have regrets? Not really.

Did I go out the way I wanted to go out? No.

Should I not have played the last year in 2012? Probably not. When you sit down and you watch the six o'clock news and you're on the news for being dropped from the Waterford panel and you know nothing about it… *I thought that was wrong.*

But yet, when they were in trouble and when they asked me back, I went back. I stayed a year too long. I probably shouldn't have gone back that time. That's one regret I'd have.

I went back.

Look, I'm after making the best mates in the world through hurling.

We had the best days. We travelled the world, literally. Everywhere… brilliant days, great memories… Argentina, Singapore, Las Vegas, Phoenix, San Francisco, Los Angeles, New York a load of times… Morocco, that was a great trip.

At the end of 2002, Sean Power was looking after the travel for us going to matches. He was in charge of Harvey Travel. We went down and said, 'Look, we didn't have a team holiday before, we're after winning Munster, can we have a team holiday?' '

'I never even thought of it, I'll talk to Justin.' Justin said that we'd go somewhere. 'Where have you in mind?'

Sean got back to him and he said the best thing you can do is go to Lanzarote for a week. You'd be guaranteed the weather... blah, blah, blah. Other counties were going to Australia and New Zealand, and we were barely getting a holiday.

Justin rings him back.

'I think we'll go to Alaska!'

'Alaska is freezing, Justin.'

Justin was mad into photography so that's why he wanted to go, to take pictures.

'Anywhere else?'

'You could go to Morocco.'

'We'll go to Morocco so!' said Justin.

This place was after being blown up about a hundred times! There was a couple of lads working in the hotel, a big, fancy hotel now so they said, 'Can we play you in a soccer match in the stadium?'

There was a football stadium a mile out the road; we passed it coming in. We were like... *Brilliant, yeah.*

'Okay, I'll organise it.'

The coach comes down, picks us up and off we go to the match. We go up by the stadium and we pass the stadium. We were like... 'No, no, no, we're playing there!'

We went into this housing estate. There were no windows on any of the apartment blocks. We started panicking now. We got up to the pitch and there was a fella with a bag of lime and he was marking out the field. It was a dirt track, there was no grass on it or nothing. *Jesus Christ almighty!*

We had some craic though! I think Justin got a goal the same night.

Ken was like a dog. Ken was injured but he wanted to play. We were due to play Dunloy in the All-Ireland semi-final with Mount Sion three weeks after we came home. They wouldn't let Ken play so he got in a strop and got a taxi back to the hotel!

We went in through a window and they made us all Moroccan tea. That was a good holiday actually. We couldn't go anywhere, we had to stay in the hotel.

The All Star trips were great. The 2002 and '03 teams went in January of 2004. We had five nights in Phoenix and three nights in Las Vegas. If it wasn't through hurling, you were never going to do that. Singapore same thing, you're never going to go to Singapore. To see all these places… Argentina. We stayed in Buenos Aires; you're never going to go there with a family. We've seen the world through hurling, we've done everything. That team. We went everywhere.

We were in Vegas. We were going home one night with a few drinks on us. You could go in and book a helicopter… *your man brings you off down the Grand Canyon and…* blah, blah, blah… 200 dollars each.

So, we paid the money. We were going the next morning.

I got up the next morning; the lads were like, 'Come on!'

'No way am I going up in a helicopter… I don't even like flying.'

'But you paid for it last night!' I didn't even remember paying for it!

Sitting in a helicopter… Fergal Hartley, Tony Browne, Ken McGrath, myself and John Mullane… flying over the Grand Canyon. That's through hurling.

You can't buy those things.

We came in and it was just gone dark. At the end of the strip was the Luxor and the MGM Grand. All the lights were on. None of us spoke for that minute.

The music was *Viva Las Vegas* by Elvis.

Ah Jesus, we had some brilliant times. Great trips. So, hurling gave me a lot.

STEPHEN MOLUMPHY

KILKENNY 2-16   WATERFORD 1-13
National Hurling League
Nowlan Park
MARCH 27, 2011

Stephen Molumphy dashed from Nowlan Park at half-time, to make a flight to Poland. His military career cut in half the Waterford captain's contribution to a vital National League encounter with Kilkenny.

★ **KILKENNY:** D Herity; M Kavanagh, N Hickey, J Dalton; T Walsh, B Hogan, JJ Delaney; E Larkin (0-1), P Hartley; A Fogarty (0-3), TJ Reid (1-2), J Mulhall; E Brennan (0-1), R Hogan (0-7), C Fennelly (1-2). Subs: PJ Delaney for Walsh, M Ruth for Mulhall, P Murphy for Hartley, C Fogarty for JJ Delaney.

★ **WATERFORD:** S O'Keeffe; D Fives, W Hutchinson, N Connors; D O'Sullivan (0-1), M Walsh, K Moran (0-1); R Foley (0-7) J Nagle; P Mahony, S Prendergast, T Ryan (0-1); J Mullane (0-1), S Walsh (1-0), **S Molumphy (0-1)**. Subs: E McGrath (0-1) for Molumphy, E Kelly for Mahony.

THE ACTION

WATERFORD CAPTAIN AND army lieutenant Stephen Molumphy answered the call of duty at half-time of this Division 1 clash. The Ballyduff Upper man got a point before he left Nowlan Park at the break due to work commitments with the Irish Defence Forces in Poland. He was still in his gear as he got into the car and left for Dublin Airport.

Kilkenny stayed in the hunt for the final as second-half goals from TJ Reid and Colin Fennelly saw off Waterford. Déise boss Davy Fitzgerald watched the match from the back of the stand after he received a four-week suspension. He was initially handed a 12-week ban following the defeat to Tipperary at Semple Stadium but it was subsequently downgraded. Selector Pat Bennett was on the sideline.

Kilkenny led 0-10 to 0-6 at half-time but lost All Star defender Tommy Walsh to injury. JJ Delaney came off in the second period.

The Déise hit the front for the first time in the 50th minute when Shane Walsh goaled from close range after Richie Foley's free came back off the post. Foley was Waterford's free-taker throughout the league campaign and finished with seven points. Sub Eoin McGrath tapped over a point to make it 1-11 to 0-12. The visitors got 1-4 without reply in the third quarter as they went from five points down to two points up.

Aidan Fogarty got a point back for the Cats before TJ Reid rose above Waterford goalkeeper Stephen O'Keeffe to turn a mishit Colin Fennelly point attempt into the net on 55 minutes.

The away side had a penalty appeal four minutes from the end when John Mullane was brought down. Referee John Sexton signalled a 20-metre free instead. Eoin Kelly went for goal but saw his shot saved and Foley flashed the rebound wide. The gap was three points deep into injury-time when Fennelly flicked another high ball past O'Keeffe.

★ ★ ★ ★ ★

66

FROM CAPTAIN BACK to Lieutenant!

I had to leave at half-time against Kilkenny in a National League match and go to work. I left early to catch my flight to Poland to complete a NATO military course for the Irish Defence Forces.

The following evening, I was sent a link to an article in the *Irish Examiner* and there was a photo included from Sportsfile. It was of myself, fully togged out in my Waterford gear, boots and all! I was getting into my car at half-time, while my wife (then girlfriend) Niamh was getting in the driver's seat because I had to race up to the airport. At the time, Davy Fitz was in charge and I was captain of the Waterford team.

My rank was Lieutenant in the military and I remember the article stated something along the lines of... *During the match, Molumphy reverted from Captain back to Lieutenant to perform his duties with the army.* I'd known for a couple of months that I had to complete this NATO course in Poland. In the Irish Defence Forces, every sailor, airman/woman and soldier must continuously upskill and expand our capabilities. This involves completing courses with armed forces across the globe.

This time it was a NATO course in the NATO Joint Force Training Centre in Bydgoszcz, Poland. In essence, it was a NATO military college and I was required to report in on Saturday or Sunday before the course commenced on Monday morning. Normally, this wasn't an issue but we had the league match on the Sunday and a chance to make the National League final so missing it wasn't an option.

Bydgoszcz in Poland is a difficult place to find a flight to from Dublin, late on a Sunday evening. I remember trying to find the latest flight from every airport, and even flights with multiple stops to try and make it work, but to no avail. The match was on in Nowlan Park which was a positive as it was closer to Dublin.

I informed Davy of the situation weeks before and he said to keep working on getting a flight. I even tried to find flights leaving in the early hours of Monday morning, but it didn't work out. After training one night, about two weeks prior to the match, Davy called me over and asked did I have any luck to which I replied with bad news. I'll never forget his response.

Quick as lightning, he said, 'What can you give me?'

We had won Munster the year before but lost in the All-Ireland semi-finals, so we were determined to push on that year. We wanted to reach the league final which required us to finish in the two top positions and we were on the way to reaching that objective.

I replied, 'Half-time and I'll have to go then.'

'Good. That's what we'll do.'

It took me by surprise but Davy knew that everyone had their commitments to work and, equally, he wanted players to empty themselves on the pitch and planned for substitutes to make a difference when introduced with a full tank of energy.

I remember constantly tackling, running, making supporting runs as much as I could for the first-half and then heading towards the dressing-room, grabbing my gear-bag at the door – one of the backroom team had it ready – and in seconds I was outside at my car. Niamh was already there waiting and we were on the motorway in minutes.

After rushing to the boarding gate in Dublin airport, I remember the flight attendant saying, 'You just made it with five minutes to spare before we closed the gate.'

I arrived over to Poland and all went to schedule.

On this NATO military course, you were not permitted to have your mobile phone inside the barracks; you had leave it behind in the hotel. When I arrived back to my hotel room on Monday evening, I had thought no one even noticed I left the match early, until I clicked on the link sent to me about the article in the *Examiner*! I was surprised to say the least.

At the end of the day, the GAA is an amateur sport but played and managed at a professional standard. We do the best we can on the field but, it's your job which pays the mortgage, takes care of your family and that takes priority.

I suppose I never actually considered missing the match! That was my third year as captain, and we wanted to win every match. We were getting stronger under Davy, as the more years you're with the same manager, the better each player knows the style and system expected of them. Despite leading in the second-half against Kilkenny, they came back and won. At the end of the 2011 National League consisting of eight teams in Division One, we finished third and Dublin and Kilkenny contested the final which Dublin won.

When Davy came to us, he was learning so much and was an excellent man-manager. He started putting structures in place and more work was done on tactical systems. Every manager has specific areas to target and it was the work-rate of the forwards in which he took a lot of interest. We were an all-out attacking team but as a forward unit, we wouldn't defend well enough. We would achieve very high scores but sometimes our opponents would score the same, if not more.

Many times it was basically a shoot-out. With Davy, the corner-forward was the first defender. He brought in that mentality that if the corner-back got around you and a score accrued later, it was your fault. He wanted more accountability from us.

The Defence Forces is an excellent organisation to be in if you like sports of any kind. They want you to represent your village or county and use the sports arena to develop your leadership skills. Regarding this match, Eoin Larkin, who was also a soldier, was playing on the Kilkenny team. Eoin was a soldier I trained.

When he came in as a recruit, I was his platoon commander. We knew each other well, were based in the same barracks in Kilkenny and played side-by-side on the 3rd Infantry Battalion hurling team against other military barracks.

The Irish Defence Forces is a fantastic place for sportsmen and sportswomen because of the similarities between team sports and what we do in the army. Everything in the military is based on mental and physical strength, loyalty, selflessness and respect. The first day I joined the army, each of us cadets were assigned to complete an individual task and I got my task done, but I was disciplined because my buddy (the soldier nearest me) failed his.

The simple lesson was, you only succeed if both of you succeed together. That was day one so while I did press-ups as the corrective action, the lesson was quickly ingrained in me. If the team wins, you win. You are only limited by your ambition and determination in the military. They are so many possibilities and different career choices that every month and every year is different.

During the 2011 season, I was based in the Military College in the Curragh, Co Kildare which was two hours from home. Looking back, the driving I did was crazy at the time. I clocked up over half a million miles on my car during those years! I needed to be at work in the Curragh for 7.45am so I would get up at 5.30am.

Large segments of the year, I was always driving in the dark, both in the morning and driving home. I would leave in the morning at 5.45am, drive for two hours to the Curragh, finish at 5pm and then drive straight down the motorway for 90 minutes to start hurling training in Waterford city, and finally 60 minutes back home to Ballyduff Upper... reaching home around 10.30pm. You can only do that for so long.

In 2014, we had our first child and the external commitments to county hurling requirements became too much. At the end of that year, I had to pull the plug. Jack was just born and in his first year I didn't see enough of him.

I had training five times a week, training camps and military exercises on and off the island, it was very time consuming. At the end of that year, I realised I couldn't give the same commitment I knew was required.

These days, you don't see too many players over 30 playing inter-county. Looking back, it was a crazy few years with a lot of ups and downs. This day was a snapshot of how busy my life was at that time, but I wouldn't change a thing! It was worth it.

MAURICE SHANAHAN

WATERFORD 3-19 CORK 1-21
Munster SHC Semi-Final
Semple Stadium
JUNE 7, 2015

After experiencing a devastating personal year in 2014, Maurice Shanahan fought back and had a magnificent year for Waterford the following summer (above, including a sublime performance against Cork in the Munster semi-final).

★ **WATERFORD:** S O'Keeffe; B Coughlan, N Connors, S Fives; A Gleeson (0-1), T De Burca (0-1), P Mahony; C Dunford (0-1), J Barron; M Walsh, K Moran (0-2), J Dillon (1-0); Stephen Bennett (0-2), **M Shanahan (1-9)**, B O'Halloran. Subs: Shane Bennett (0-2) for O'Halloran, T Devine (1-0) for Stephen Bennett, E Barrett for Dunford, P Curran (0-1) for Dillon.

★ **CORK:** A Nash; S O'Neill, S McDonnell, B Murphy; D Cahalane, M Ellis (0-1), C Murphy; D. Kearney (0-1), B Cooper (0-1); C Lehane (0-1), P Cronin (0-5), A Walsh (0-1); A Cadogan (0-2), P Horgan (1-7), L O'Farrell (0-1). Subs: R O'Shea for C Murphy, D McCarthy (0-1) for Kearney, P O'Sullivan for Walsh.

THE ACTION

WATERFORD COMPLETED A league and championship double over Cork to reach a first Munster final in three years.

Pauric Mahony suffered a horrendous broken leg on club duty for Ballygunner just six days after the league final win over the Rebels. He was top scorer in that campaign with 1-90.

In his absence, Maurice Shanahan stepped up with 1-9. It was a remarkable year for Shanahan who had stepped off the panel in 2014 due to mental health issues, which culminated in a suicide attempt.

Shanahan went on to shoot 2-38 in the 2015 championship and finished the season with his first All Star. Later in the year, he spoke to WLR sports reporter Kevin Casey in an emotional interview about his battle with depression and his attempts to take his own life during 2014. He withdrew from the Waterford panel that summer but with the help of family, friends and club-mates, he returned for 2015.

Waterford were slow out of the blocks and trailed Jimmy Barry-Murphy's side by six points to two after 21 minutes. They also hit eight wides. A goal from Man of the Match Shanahan on 27 minutes brought them to life. The Lismore man caught an Austin Gleeson delivery over Damien Cahalane and found the top corner of the net past the flying hurley of Anthony Nash.

Three minutes later, Michael Walsh sent Jake Dillon through on goal and he fired home to leave it 2-6 to 0-11 to the league champions at the break.

Shanahan struck five second-half points. A Patrick Horgan penalty in injury-time reduced the deficit to two before Déise sub Tom Devine goaled at the other end, just as he did in the league final. Walsh was again the supplier.

★ ★ ★ ★ ★

"

WE GOT ONTO the bus to head into Semple Stadium and Pauric Mahony wasn't on the bus; we didn't really cop it to be honest with you. He went with the backroom team in the car.

Under Derek McGrath, we always watched videos of us training and things like that. The video came on and at the end of the video, as we were just coming into Semple Stadium, Paudie came on the video and he spoke. It was an emotional video; he kind of broke down. When I looked around, Austin Gleeson was beside me and Philip Mahony was in front of me. There were nearly tears in everyone's eyes getting off the bus.

I think it was Kevin Moran who stood up and said, 'We have to do it for Pauric today!' It hit home what a loss Pauric Mahony was to us. In my eyes, he is definitely one of the best hurlers in Ireland. The video was wicked emotional.

We got off and went in into the dressing-room and Pauric was in there and people went over to him. The biggest thing Pauric wanted was for us to perform on the day and win the match, so we had to concentrate on that again.

Before the match, I was practicing a few frees and he was there beside me hobbling on the crutches, unfortunately, but he was there and he was giving me a bit of advice. When you have someone like Pauric Mahony giving you advice like that... we all know what a free-taker he is! In my eyes, he is more than a free-taker because everything goes through him and what a loss he was for us that day.

He said, 'If you miss the first one, hit the second one... hit the third one!' The bit of advice he gave me was... *If they go over, they go over... but that's gone, you have to move on to the next one. If you get eight of them, eight of them might go over but it's always the next one... always the next one.* That's what I got from him that day.

It was a great help because I actually missed the first one! I was kind of saying... *Oh Jesus...* because it wasn't a hard one either and it was my first year on the frees so it was important for me to get a good start, but I didn't and it went wide. I just remembered in my own head what Pauric said... *The next one, the next one.*

Thankfully, after that, I didn't miss any.

Three weeks before that, I got injured playing against Cappoquin in a club championship game over in Ballyduff. When I came out of that game, it was touch and go. I went to Waterford Regional Hospital the Monday after the match and they thought my cruciate was gone. I rang Derek and to be fair to Derek, he rang Tadhg O'Sullivan straight away and I went straight from Waterford Regional to Whitfield to Tadhg.

Thankfully, Tadhg looked at the scan and looked at my knee that afternoon, and he said, 'No, your cruciate is not gone, it's just badly swollen and badly bruised on your kneecap which could take a few weeks... so your cruciate is definitely not gone!' It was a blessing.

Then, we went away to Johnstown House on a training camp nearly two weeks before the Cork game and I didn't train at all. I did a lot of free-taking alright with Tony Óg Regan from Galway. He was in helping the team that time. Tony was a good man and he was good to get in your head and give me a few tips.

That's all I was really doing. Only 10 days before the Cork game, I went back out onto the field, back training with the lads and doing my own stuff really. Only for the Tuesday and Thursday of the Cork game, I trained properly with the lads and I remember on the Thursday night, our physio Conor McCarthy said to me, 'You definitely won't last the 70 minutes, it's not possible for you to last the 70 minutes!'

I did a lot of work inside in the gym: a lot of cardio work, bike work, rowing and that kind of stuff. I wasn't a hundred percent but I felt in a good place in my own body and in my own head. That's half the battle.

I had a lot of meetings with Tony going into those games. He said, 'Once your head is right, things will go.' I missed the first free on the day but I caught a ball after that off Cormac Murphy and when I caught the ball I thought... *I'm on here!* You know yourself and I knew... *I'm on here for a good one.*

Thankfully, it worked out like that.

Tony was helping around five or six players. Whoever wanted to go to him... some people believe in that stuff and other people don't. Whoever wanted to go to him, went to him. He definitely helped me. The one thing I lacked was a bit of confidence. Back then, Tony helped me big-time.

Austin Gleeson hit in the ball and I remember being up in the air and Damien Cahalane was in front of me around 30 yards out from goal. I played his hurley big-time, to be honest with you! Once you're cute you won't get caught doing that I suppose! I picked it up from Dan down through the years.

The minute I got the ball in my hand, I went for it. I took off on a solo run and Jake Dillon was just inside me. If I missed it, Derek would have killed me! I could have hand-passed into Jake but I let fly from around 21-yards and it went straight into the top corner.

I remember turning around, running back out to wing forward… it brought a lot of emotion to me to get that goal because of what I went through the year before. I remember running back out and I gave a fist pump to the crowd and Derek said, 'You're time is now kid, you're after arriving'.

That's one thing that always stuck with me from that game. When you hear that from your manager, it gives you a big boost. I clenched my fist and there were tears in my eyes. It was something I needed; I needed a big performance. Since I started, I was in and out of teams. I needed that goal and I kicked on for the rest of the year from that.

After that, things went well, I got a few more frees, one or two from play; I ended up with 1-9. The most important thing that day was Waterford winning. We all did it for Pauric. Some of the management and players had his initials on our hands. The one thing about Derek McGrath's teams, it wasn't about individuals, it was about the team and the panel of players we had.

Tom Devine came on that day and he got a goal near the end. It was a fantastic day for us and a big day for Derek as well because the boys lost to Wexford the year before. It was great to get back into a Munster final.

The first fella I went to after that game was Pauric. The minute we embraced each other, I said, 'It was for you kid!' He said, 'No it was for the team!'

He drove the team on. I know he was off the field but leaders like him don't come around too often. When they're off the field, you still listen to them. He's definitely up there with one of the best hurlers I ever played with.

The All Star meant a lot to me.

My best year playing for Waterford was 2015. Like anyone would say, I'd swap that in the morning if it meant Waterford would be All-Ireland champions. Unfortunately, it didn't work out like that, but 2015 definitely was a good year.

When I was playing with Lismore in underage games and going on to play with Blackwater Community School, I was always Dan's younger brother. The one thing Dan said to me was, 'You're your own person!'

When I was 15 of 16, Dan said, 'People are going to be saying that but don't let it get into your head'. He gave me that kind of advice.

'I'm Dan, you're Maurice… we're two different people!' That kind of stuff. The one thing I took from watching Dan was… Dan was a slow starter, he tried for four or five years before he hit his peak. Dan never gave up on his journey and on his training with Waterford. He knew if he kept at it that he would perform to the best of his ability.

In 2007, he got Hurler of the Year and it was a great privilege for himself, but for us as a family as well. As a young lad, when I was watching Dan and watching Waterford teams losing, the criticism they were getting was absolutely crazy from Waterford supporters, and everywhere to be honest. To be in the stand, listening to that.

When I went on to play with Waterford, I had to block all of that out and believe in myself. You have bad days in matches but if you know you're after putting in the work and that kind of stuff, you know the day will come that it's all going to turn for you. Thankfully, it did for me.

With Dan as a selector, I got no favouritism to be honest with you! There was many a day when I wasn't starting! Since I've been playing senior with Lismore, I've been involved with Dan. It wasn't a hindrance to me at all. For a brother to be involved as a selector, I embraced it in a good way. I could go and say, 'What can I do to get better?'

He was at training every night saying to make a run in from No 10, and come in behind the way he used to. It wasn't just to me; he was telling every forward. To get the advice from Dan was a good thing for me. When Dan left, it was a big hole left there for me because I didn't have him to fall back on. It was never a hindrance.

If I was good enough to be playing, if I was performing in training, I was playing… and if wasn't, then I wasn't playing.

Dan has been a massive influence on my life like my other brother James in Australia and my two sisters as well. On the hurling field, Dan was my biggest influence to be honest with you. I could always go to him and talk to him. He would tell me what I was doing right but he would also tell me what I had to improve on.

Even before that Cork game in 2015, he rang me one Monday evening.

'Where are you?'

'I'm at home.'

'I'll meet you in the field in a half an hour.'

I went up and he said, 'Stand in full-forward there!'... and he told me what runs to make. 'Bring him out and bring him back in!'

That kind of stuff helped me big-time. He has done it all and I was trying to get to that peak.

Even off the field, in 2014 Dan would have been around for me a lot like all my family. He brought me to matches; Lismore would have been playing challenge matches so I went with Dan. He was probably afraid to leave me out of his sight at the time. Thankfully, he didn't and thankfully, we're here to talk about it as well.

From a very young age in Lismore, I looked up to Sean Prendergast. He did a load for Lismore hurling and still does to this day. If you ask me, apart from my family, he was the biggest influence on my career. From the day we walked into the Primary School in Lismore to this day, Sean is involved. When you have people like him in a club, it's very easy to keep going back. He was a big influence on my career and even in 2014, he would have called to me many a day after school, nearly every day for two or three weeks after school. He was manager of the senior hurling team in Lismore at the time.

Derek McGrath was a good man to me as well off the field. In 2014, I pulled off the panel. Derek still involved me. Even when I wasn't there, he was texting me and that kind of stuff. If the lads got gear, I still got the gear at home.

I wouldn't have been in and around the circle at all but when they lost to Wexford in Nowlan Park, I remember I got a text... *You're with us next year kid.* When I got that text, it meant a lot to me. To try and get back on the Waterford panel and knowing you're wanted was a big thing. Derek was very good to me. Brendan Landers as well, all the Prendergasts in Lismore; the name itself will tell you what hurling people they are.

The community of Lismore, the Lismore GAA club, I could name them all to be honest with you. The players I played with and still to this day, they're the people I really have to thank. The community of Lismore and wider to Waterford and even wider to that again. It's been phenomenal the amount of support I got off people.

Off the field, I have to go away and talk to counsellors and that kind of stuff. They've all helped me, talking to people. The GPA helped me greatly. Anything I needed, I just picked up the phone and rang the GPA. They'd have a fella to meet you in the morning. Things like that, people wouldn't see. People mightn't even know that the GPA do that kind of stuff. It's absolutely phenomenal work that they do.

I would love to play for Waterford again. It might be too late for me. To be honest with you, I'm fitter than I was a few years ago which is strange because with this pandemic, I'm training away mad. I'm loving going to the hurling field. I'm loving that and I'm loving training. I train four or five nights a week. If I got called back, it would be something I'd have to think about. Then again, who knows.

BETH CARTON

WATERFORD 3-10 MEATH 3-9
All-Ireland Intermediate Championship Semi-Final
Nowlan Park
AUGUST 22, 2015

Beth Carton (centre) celebrates with Deirdre Brennan and Niamh Rockett after Waterford's All-Ireland Intermediate victory in 2015, though it was the comeback against Meath in the semi-final that year that lives with Beth.

★ **WATERFORD:** D Brennan; K McMahon, C Whyte, V Falconer; C Raher, J Simpson (0-1), I Heffernan; P Jackman (0-5), L Bray (0-1); N Morrissey, N Rockett (0-1), **B Carton (1-1)**; A Power (1-0), C McGlone, D Power. Subs: B Kavanagh for Morrissey, S Curran (1-1) for D Power, V O'Brien for J Simpson, J Simpson for A Power.

★ **MEATH:** E Mangan; E Coffey, C Coffey, G Coleman; A Keogh, K Troy, L O'Donoghue; A Maguire, K Hackett; S Hackett (0-1), E Guy, A Minogue (0-3); M Thynne (1-0), J Dolan (2-5), C O'Brien. Subs: A Gaffney for Guy, M Keogh for E Coffey, F O'Brien for Gaffney, A Thompson for Thynne.

THE ACTION

WATERFORD CLAWED THEIR way back from nine points down to pip Meath in an epic All-Ireland intermediate camogie semi-final.

Sean Fleming's side trailed by 3-5 to 0-5 after 33 minutes but second-half goals by Shona Curran, Aisling Power and Beth Carton utterly changed the complexion of the contest. The Déise defended heroically over seven minutes of stoppage time to set up a Croke Park date with Kildare.

They endured a first-half from hell, where Meath full-forward Jane Dolan rocked them with 2-3. Waterford's MVP Patricia Jackman had one of her finest hours. The Gailltír leader showed up all over the field to galvanise the troops especially when they were struggling. She put her body on the line to outmuscle opponents and win possession. She raised five white flags (three frees and two from play).

Beth Carton came alive when moved into the inside line for the second-half. Her debut season was one to remember. The talented teenager was an All-Ireland medallist and a Soaring Star recipient by the end of the year. In defence, Claire Whyte, Charlotte Raher and Kate McMahon cleared a pile of ball when Meath searched for an equaliser in stoppage time. Iona Heffernan dealt with Dolan after her early splurge.

★★★★★

❝

THE CROWD IS the one thing I'll never forget from that day.

It's probably the only time I've heard a crowd at a camogie game chanting the Waterford chant that you would hear at a hurling game. In the second-half, when we were coming back and near the end, I could hear that… whoever got it going!

That was a big thing from it, the crowd was so good. Obviously, it was a lot of our families and that too. In the second-half, we got momentum and you could see that slowly we were starting to claw it back.

I remember we were in a ruck by our '45', we were up by a point, and everyone was just saying, 'Keep it in the ruck… don't let it come out!' We were out on our feet and if the ball came out, it could have broken, so it was important to keep it in the ruck at that stage.

When the whistle went, it was just pure elation. Knowing your season is still there. I think semi-finals are the worst place to lose; they are literally there just to be won. We had a great year. We had a few tough early morning training sessions under Brother Philip Ryan. It was just everything coming together. It was pure relief too in a way because it looked at half-time that the season was nearly over.

At half-time, the management just said we had 30 minutes to try and hold on to that season. It's either 30 minutes to get to a final… or a whole year to even try to get back to that spot… to half-time in a semi-final, so that was a big thing.

Literally, 30 minutes… Give it absolutely everything and whatever happens at the end of that, at least you can go out with your head held high. With a lot of us being in our first year, we probably didn't cop it as much but a lot of the older girls really empathised with it. I remember Trish Jackman talking going out and just saying how hard it is to get back there. They had been beaten in previous semi-finals and they knew how hard it was.

Shona Curran made a big difference and when she got that goal, it settled us and we were kind of like… *Okay, we can go here and play our own game.* That first goal was massive and then the others followed.

Our backs started to get on top. Iona Heffernan was on Jane Dolan, who is a serious, *serious* player and they just started winning ball there and we started scoring up the other end.

My mam and my dad were there that day and my little sister. My mam is nervous enough watching the matches. When we were up by the point near the end, she was up the back with Aisling Power's mam; the two of them weren't even watching it because they couldn't! My auntie was there as well, she goes to a lot of the matches and my grandad was there too. He always went to the games.

The last game he was at was the 2015 final so that year was a big one. I visit him before all the big games. I call for a chat and get some advice... or a lecture!

My dad was at every single game up to Covid. My mam finds them a bit more difficult to watch even still! She remembers that one alright!

Any advice I need, my dad is definitely the first person I go to. On anything. He's the first person to criticise you when you need it but when you need a pat on the back or a lift, he's there as well. He's had such an influence on my career.

He's the reason I'm playing and I've been able to constantly improve.

I played with the boys up to under-10. It was where I got a chance to really develop my skills. I was trying to be as strong as them and hurl as quickly as them. It benefitted me in a way as well. What I remember from those times is the Friday night leagues, going up to Cleaboy and Gracedieu. It was something I always really looked forward to. The toughest games were always against Mount Sion and Roanmore, the rival clubs. There was no holding back no matter whether you were a girl or a boy! That's the way it should be.

Another good memory was the Roanmore blitz; I always loved playing in that every year. It used to be on a Saturday, a day-blitz where all the clubs from everywhere came down. It was on in Roanmore and De La Salle. It was a real day out. It was under-8 and ground hurling. I don't why but it's always a memory that sticks out.

We set up the camogie team in De La Salle in 2008 when I was 10. There were a few girls playing with the boys who had brothers and we were getting to the age where we couldn't keep playing. So, it was either go play with someone else or give it a go ourselves. I played camogie and basketball growing up. I really did love basketball. It was played in the winter and the camogie was played in the summer so they complemented each other until I got to a certain age where there was no off-season for the camogie or the basketball. I would always have gone the camogie route, even though I loved the basketball.

It probably has helped me develop some skills for the camogie and it did give me that outlet away from the camogie. We played a lot in the Presentation Secondary School. I'm disappointed that I did have to give it up but it just got to a stage, especially playing college camogie, that it wasn't feasible to do both to the standard I wanted to. I was 18 when I stepped away from the basketball.

One of my heroes was John Mullane with the club. When you have someone that close to home who is doing so well and doing something that you love… and to see him up in the pitch midweek was massive. What he used to do at the weekends for Waterford was phenomenal. Even looking now at the level of commitment he's still putting into the club and the camogie club. He is still such a role model.

My dad brought me to the camogie games a lot and a big one for me growing up was watching Ursula Jacob. I remember we went to the Wexford-Cork All-Ireland final in 2012… *and her goal from the ground!* What that Wexford team did in that period outside of the Corks and the Kilkennys was phenomenal… its something that I'd be looking at and hoping someday that the breakthrough is possible. I got a goal from a free in the All-Ireland final against Kildare but it was actually a mishit! A few people thought afterwards that it was intentional and I left them thinking a bit! I was just so lucky. I remember Nicola Morrissey was standing in front of it and she turned to me and she was like, 'You could have told me you were going for it!' *I didn't know myself!*

It meant a lot to become Waterford's first All Star. I'd be a firm believer that I wouldn't be getting any of those awards without all the girls, especially when you're in the full-forward line and you're hitting the frees. For my family, it was a lovely moment. They were able to have that night. My dad brought me to everything until I got my own car! They were literally like taxi drivers!

Little things like that you think back to. When you're not going well or you're form isn't great after losing a game, they're the ones that have to put up with that. My mam would have been cooking the dinners and washing the gear, and stuff like that. It was nice for the family to have a night like that and enjoy it. For Waterford camogie in general, it was a big one. Those accolades are more for the people around you that have helped you to get there rather than yourself.

PATRICIA JACKMAN

WATERFORD 2-9 KILDARE 1-5
All-Ireland Intermediate Championship Final
Croke Park
SEPTEMBER 13, 2015

Patricia Jackman competing in the All-Ireland Poc Fada in Louth in 2014, the year before she experienced championship glory with Waterford in Croke Park.

★ **WATERFORD:** D Brennan; K McMahon, C Whyte, V Falconer; C Raher, J Simpson (0-1), I Heffernan; **P Jackman (0-1)**, C McGlone; N Morrissey (0-1), N Rockett (0-1), B Carton (1-2); A Power (1-0), L Bray (0-3), D Power. Subs: S Curran for D Power, V O'Brien for Rockett, N Rockett for Morrissey, C Murphy for McGlone, D Power for A Power.

★ **KILDARE:** R O'Connell; C Flanagan, C Nolan, F Trant; A Lyons, R Gorman, C Farrell; C Forde, O Bambury; S Hurley, N Earley (1-0), L Keatley; E Reilly (0-2), S O'Carroll (0-2), M Lyons (0-1). Subs: H McDonnell for Forde, D Byrne for Trant.

THE ACTION

CAITHRIONA MCGLONE LED the girls in blue up the Hogan Stand steps to collect the Jack McGrath Cup for the very first time.

Goals either side of the break by Aisling Power and Beth Carton turned this final in their favour. Power's hard earned green flag on 29 minutes sent Waterford into the lead for the very first time. There was an element of good fortune about the second as Beth Carton's free from the left wing skidded past three Kildare bodies and nestled in the corner of the net.

Bundle of energy Lorraine Bray earned the Player of the Match gong. The diminutive No 9 knocked over three points from five shots, including two second-half efforts.

After trailing by five points in the first quarter, shrewd tactical moves changed the course of this game. Patricia Jackman moved to centre-back, in a swap with Jennie Simpson, and slipped seamlessly into the sweeper role. Waterford endured a nightmare start as the rain poured down on Jones' Road. Noelle Early palmed the ball high to the Hill 16 net after just two minutes. Melissa Lyons and Emer Reilly added Kildare points as Waterford hit five wides into the Canal End.

Beth Carton got a badly needed point off her favoured left side on 14 minutes and followed that up with a free. With 29 minutes on the clock, Curran cursed her luck after her point effort dropped around the goalmouth. Aisling Power caught the sliotar but let it slip out of her grasp. She regained possession, however, and belted the ball past Roisin O'Connell as Waterford led 1-4 to 1-2 at half time.

Another bolt from the blue arrived early in the second period. Seventeen-year-old Carton stood over a dead ball to the left of the posts and her low strike caught the Kildare defence unawares. Her sixth goal of the championship. Waterford were on their way to the senior ranks.

★★★★★

"

THERE WAS AN eerie silence at times in Croke Park that day. Because of the weather, the crowd had actually retreated to the back of the stand. I do remember literally at one stage hearing the water running through the drains underneath Croke Park!

It was a bizarre moment! It just felt that eerily quiet.

It was a tough game against Kildare but we found our feet after 20 or 25 minutes. Aisling Power managed to find enough space to get a shot at goal and we were able to get into half-time ahead and we hadn't necessarily played as well as we could. When we went out in the second-half, everyone just came alive, Beth Carton got the goal and Lorraine Bray really caught fire, as she tends to do in every single game!

It was great to see a lot of the younger players come through and equally for the players who had been there for a long time. I'm thinking about players like Jennie Simpson, Charlotte Raher, Shona Curran, Niamh Rockett, Nicola Morrissey, Jenny McCarthy and Claire Whyte… players who had been there from the junior days and now they had helped us get to the senior ranks. And for a lot of players up in the stand, who weren't with us on the pitch, they were just as much a part of the journey of getting to a day like that. My club-mate Emma Hannon moved to Australia a few months previously; she sent us her best wishes and some welcome advice.

That year, in general, there was a sense of change. A new era.

I recall a game we played against Tipperary in WIT. In the warm-up, we had new players and there was a sense that there was something different and that carried on throughout the year. We were undefeated in the National League and the championship.

When I was at the bottom of the steps of the Hogan Stand, I looked up and I saw people that mean a lot to me. Shane 'Shiner' Ahearne was in tears at one stage and he waved down. I saw Tony and Helen Cummins as well. I had an idea of where they might be. I looked up and got the wave, so they're moments I'll never forget.

Coming back onto the Quay in Waterford and meeting people in the Granville

Hotel was very special. I got to meet my family, my friends and I remember there was a huge contingent of Gailltír underage players. At the time, I was actually the only player from the club on the county team. Just even looking back at the photo now of all those players, there was probably 10 or 12 of them that went on to win a club All-Ireland a few years later so that was special.

And meeting people who were part of the journey, Lilian O'Sullivan in particular. I still recall Lilian in 2003, one of the former Waterford players, who was in O'Moore Park in Portlaoise to see Waterford win a first All-Ireland, the under-16 B; and the thrill to see players from her generation that were there that day is something I'll never forget. That was 99 years of the Camogie Association and Waterford had never won an All-Ireland. To meet someone like her in the Granville that evening was definitely very special.

I was studying at the University of Lincoln that year. It was very challenging. Number one, I had to organise my own training. I had no one to train with and I didn't have a trainer so that was obviously very challenging; and fitting that around study and work.

And then, the travel. I had to organise all my own travel.

At the time, I didn't have a car so I was relying on public transport; trains and buses. I was quite lucky for a bit of that year that Waterford Airport was still operating so I was occasionally able to get a flight into Birmingham and the difference that made was huge. Most of the time, I was flying from Birmingham to Dublin. Three hours to get to Birmingham, fly over to Dublin… and get the bus down to Waterford. Door-to-door, it was 10 or 11 hours. It was very draining.

The second year I tried to do it, it definitely took its toll. It's not sustainable for a long period of time and I wouldn't recommend it. Trying to recover after that was something that I didn't do so well. I just felt that when I was back I wanted to train. There was that element of feeling guilty that I wasn't training. When there was a younger team there, I felt that it was important to be a leader.

Gym access was fine. I'd be up into the gym for half six and done by a quarter to eight. Some mornings, it would be running. If it involved skills, there wasn't too much more I could do other than hit a sliotar off a wall. That was pretty much what it came down to. I managed a find a wall at the back of some stores in Lincoln!

I did get a couple of strange looks and the odd police vehicle slowing down going past! I was spotted once or twice and my colleagues took a couple of pictures. They did think it was rather odd.

That's what I tended to do. If I needed to do speed-work, there was a park where I could do that, or sometimes I ran on a green area at the university campus. The biggest thing that I missed was the physical contact. That's something that you just can't replicate. Even though there were a couple of days where I got someone to hold a tackle bag, you're still not replicating some of those movements. That was certainly something that was lost but I tried to do my best with the other elements.

My colleagues were really interested; a lot of them were curious. They have watched the games over the years and have always been really supportive. The very fact I was doing something quite different definitely intrigued people. Whether it's devising strength and conditioning plans or giving me some advice, my colleagues have always been really helpful.

I started with the senior county team in my Junior Cert year. I was playing basketball at the time at a high level with the school. We were Division A at the time and got to the All-Ireland final. I was trying to manage playing under-16, minor and senior with the county and the same with the club, and the basketball as well, so I had to learn pretty quickly how to manage my study alongside my sport.

I also wanted to do well in my study. There was never a trade-off, I wanted to do well in both. It was as simple as that. In later years, if there was anything I could pass onto the younger players with their studying, I was keen to do so. I just wanted to help them in some way; they were the ones who did all the work.

I started playing camogie at the tail-end of 1998 when I was seven, so compared to when players start now, I was a bit of a late starter! I always had a hurley at home, a basketball and a basketball hoop which I think was a piece of a hose that was screwed onto a washing line! The Waterford Wildcats, at that time, were the top team in the country and being a basketball player was definitely on the radar. I had my first session with Tony Cummins in the Ursuline hall and Aileen, his daughter, was helping. He spotted that I was new and I remember we were doing the roll-lift and he said I might need a little help with that because I hadn't moved on to anything like that.

Aileen took me down to the corner and she helped me.

I had Tony coaching me for the bones of 17 or 18 years with the club. There's no two ways about it, he was my most influential coach. It's only now, when I'm on the other side, that I look back and I recognise the pearls of wisdom that he bestowed on me. At the time, he would have always said to me that I should smile a bit more. Maybe a few others would say it as well! In a good way!

Tony always said that the mornings training out in Ballymabin would be the best days and not to let our careers pass us by. When you start to get a little bit older, those things start to mean a lot to you.

I was very lucky in the club that we were always encouraged to watch camogie. Now, we talk a lot about… *If you can't see it, you can't be it.* I was very lucky that I was part of a club where we were always encouraged to watch players. We heard stories about the Downeys. I watched the Tipperary camogie team; that was the team we aspired to be like. The Una O'Dwyers, the Ciara Gaynors… these were the players that Tony was talking to us about in the field, in addition to the Paul Flynns and the Fergal Hartleys, of course!

It was camogie we were there to play and he wanted us to have those female role models to look up to. Sometimes I saw Sinead Nealon up in Ballygunner training on her own, which was also very inspiring.

I started with the Ballygunner boys' teams when I was under-11 and I played until under-14. It was amazing. I tended to play two age-groups. I started at my own age group and I was a substitute at the age group above it. We got to two Féiles, reaching the semi-finals in 2004. That was a tremendous experience, just to be part of that. When you look back at the photos of the team… Stephen O'Keeffe, Barry Coughlan, Pauric Mahony, Philip Mahony and Brian O'Sullivan… it's phenomenal to look at that group and think that I was playing alongside them.

There were a lot of things I picked up. I still remember one of my first sessions with Mick Mahony. I was chasing after one of the boys and I was trying to hook him but he said, 'You need to get around him and try and block him'. I started to learn fairly quickly that there were more effective ways of doing things. That was good because it challenged me in different ways. I played in the forwards which was a bit different to where I eventually ended up. I picked up so many skills just from watching the boys.

Philip Mahony had an exceptional dummy hand-pass, so I tried to pick that up! When I look back on it, you couldn't buy that type of experience. The people who worked with us were fantastic; we had Mick Mahony, Liam Murphy, Pascal Moore, Eugene Duggan, Noel O'Keeffe and Pat Flynn. They were just exceptional people. I was never treated any different; I was there and they wanted me to be a good player. Whether I was a girl or a boy, it didn't matter. I revelled in that as well!

Some of the most competitive matches I ever played were out in the front garden! It would have been myself, Úna and Thomas out hurling. That's where some of the competitiveness came from. Ciara came along then and she was able to show us how it was done too. To play with your sisters is very special. We're fairly grounded as well.

My parents have been very supportive. You'd see dad and mam out at the games. Dad would have always been the one driving us to training and agreeing to taking 10 shots in the front garden, knowing full well that pucking around in the garden never lasted only 10 shots. Equally mam has been there and given us a huge amount of help at home in preparation.

With the Poc Fada, dad was hugely involved. He was the one identifying where to aim my shots, judging the wind and giving me a word of reassurance as well if I was a bit annoyed with the shot! When I was practicing for the county or Munster, I did a trial run around the courses. We had a fair idea of what the yardage would be and he would walk 80 or 90 yards and stand where I was aiming for.

If there was a breeze, he would adjust his line. No different to having a caddy in golf, he was helping me! The family had a bag with tea and biscuits when I got over half-way before we turned to come back. There were always some refreshments on the course!

I call Lincoln a home away from home! My home *home* is Waterford and always will be. There's nothing to say that further on in life that won't change. Things are going well in the job and it gives me a chance to challenge myself from a professional perspective. I enjoy what I do here; I've been here for seven years now which is hard to believe considering that I had never lived away from home before I came!

I teach Sport and Exercise Psychology. In my role, I also undertake a lot of research. I educate students on how they can use psychology to influence participation, welfare, well-being and performance in sports and physical activity. I give them guidance on how to construct a teaching environment or a coaching environment that is going to bring about positive psychological outcomes such as boosting confidence, helping people become more motivated or making it really enjoyable.

Alongside that, I do a lot of research particularly around optimal experience. My area of expertise would be around how people have these rewarding experiences, how they can elevate their performance under pressure and how we can help athletes and exercisers to cope with those type of situations.

I do a lot of work here in Lincoln in that area from a research perspective in collaboration with other researchers in the UK, Ireland and Australia.

MORE
GREAT
SPORTS BOOKS
FROM
HEROBOOKS

www.**HERO**BOOKS.digital

TIPPERARY
GAME OF MY LIFE

THE GREATEST TIPPERARY hurlers over the last 50 years remember the one game in blue and gold that defined their lives...

Jimmy Finn, Theo English, Tony Wall, Tadhg O'Connor, Dinny Ryan, Babs Keating, John Sheedy, Ken Hogan, Colm Bonnar, Cormac Bonnar, Declan Carr, Michael Cleary, Pat Fox, Conal Bonnar, Declan Ryan, Michael Ryan, Joe Hayes, Eamonn Corcoran, Tommy Dunne, Shane McGrath, James Woodlock, Brendan Cummins, Eoin Kelly, Michael Cahill, Brendan Maher, James Barry, Seamus Callinan and more...

A game that will live with each man forever.

Author: Stephen Gleeson
Print Price: €20.00
Ebook: €10.00
ISBN: 9781910827185

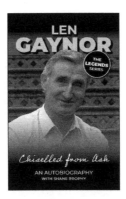

Chiselled from Ash
Len Gaynor: An Autobiography

CHISELLED FROM ASH is a story of love and honour.

It's the story of Len Gaynor's great love for the game of hurling, and how he has honoured the great game his whole life.

Len Gaynor won it all with Tipperary, finishing his career with three All-Ireland hurling titles, four Munster titles and two National League titles in the 1960s and 70s. But the flamboyant wing back also wanted to give back at the end of his career.

The Kilruane MacDonaghs clubman - and winner of three county titles - quickly proved himself to be one of the smartest and most ambitious coaches in the game.

At club level he strived to teach and help the next generation, and led his own Kilruane and neighbouring clubs to success – and at county level through the 1990s Len Gaynor managed Tipperary and Clare on the biggest stages in the game.

Chiselled from Ash is the story of one man's great love for a great game that has remained undimmed over seven decades.

Authors: Len Gaynor with Shane Brophy
Print Price: €20.00
Ebook: €10.00
ISBN: 9781910827208

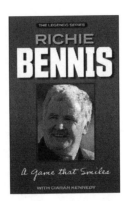

'A Game that Smiles'
The Richie Bennis Autobiography

RICHIE BENNIS IS one of the true legends remaining in the game of hurling. A towering figure in Limerick GAA, he played a central role as the county won the All-Ireland title in 1973 and then he strived as hard as anyone to see the Liam MacCarthy Cup return to the Treaty County.

It was a wait of 45 years – during which time Bennis worked at grassroots hurling in the famed Patrickswell club, where he hurled into his 40s and won 10 county titles. He also led Limerick as team manager to the 2007 All-Ireland final where they lost to Kilkenny.

In 2018, Limerick were crowned All-Ireland champions.

For Richie Bennis, a long agonising wait ended. His story is one of triumph, and heartache and personal tragedy, and a courage that was never dimmed.

Authors: Richie Bennis with Ciarán Kennedy
Print Price: €20.00
ISBN: 9781910827093

Available on
Amazon
Apple Books
Kobo
And all good book shops

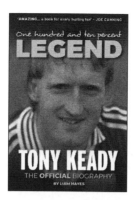

One Hundred and Ten Percent Legend
Tony Keady: The Official Biography

WHEN TONY KEADY died suddenly in August of 2017, at just 53 years of age, a whole county mourned and the rest of the country stopped in its tracks to say goodbye to a legend of the game of hurling.

Except Tony Keady was more than a legend.

In 1988, after leading Galway to a second All-Ireland title in succession, he was crowned the greatest hurler in Ireland. He was 25 years of age and there was nobody like him, nobody to touch him in the maroon No.6 shirt.

But, four years later, and still not 30, after being wrongly banned for 12 months by the GAA, he was also discarded by his own county and refused a maroon jersey the very last time he walked out onto Croke Park behind the Galway team.

A few months before his death, Tony Keady visited Liam Hayes and told him he wished to tell his own story. He felt it was time, but tragically time was not on Tony's side. One month after he died Galway won the All-Ireland title for the first time since 1988, and 80,000 people rose from their seats in the sixth minute of the game to applaud and remember a man who was more than a legend

Tony's wife, Margaret and his daughter, Shannon and his three boys, Anthony, Harry and Jake, decided to finish telling the story of a father and a hurler who always asked those around him for '110%.

Author: Liam Hayes
Price: €20.00
ISBN: 9781910827048

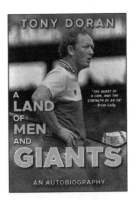

A Land of Men and Giants
The Tony Doran Autobiography

WEXFORD'S ALL-IRELAND winning hero Tony Doran was a giant in the game of hurling through the 1960s, 70s and 80s, at a time when full-forwards were ordered to plunder goals.

In his 19 years and 187 appearances as a Wexford hurler, Tony Doran successfully went for goal 131 times.

But Doran also played against giants from Kilkenny, Tipperary and Cork, and so many other counties, at a time when the game of hurling tested the wits and the courage of every man on the field.

Some of these men became giants.

A Land of Men and Giants is the story told by Tony Doran of a life spent living and competing against legendary men and true giants of the game.

A Land of Men and Giants: The Autobiography of Tony Doran is edited by award-winning writer and author Liam Hayes.

Authors: Tony Doran with Liam Hayes
Print Price: €20.00
ISBN: 9781910827031

Available on
Amazon

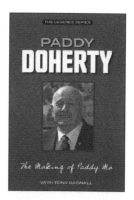

The Making of Paddy Mo
Paddy Doherty: An Autobiography

TO THIS DAY, Down's Paddy Doherty is still remembered as one of the most lethal finishers in the history of Gaelic football. The Ballykinlar clubman was fast, and breathtaking on the ball.

He led his county to a long awaited All-Ireland victory in 1960, and the following summer he captained the Mournemen and brought the Sam Maguire Cup back across the border a second time.

Doherty continued to rip apart defences throughout the decade and won a third All-Ireland crown with Down in 1968, when the Mournemen defeated Kerry in September for the second time, to add to seven Ulster titles and three National league titles.

The 1960s was a decade which is best remembered for the legend of Paddy Doherty.

And... The Making of Paddy Mo.

Authors: Paddy Doherty with Tony Bagnall
Print Price: €20.00
Ebook: €10.00
ISBN: 9781910827178

Available on
Amazon
Apple Books
Kobo
And all good online stores

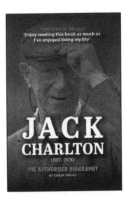

Jack Charlton
The Authorised Biography

AS ONE OF the true legends of Irish and English football, Jack Charlton was a man both loved and feared, but now the people who have lived with him all of his life introduce the real 'Big Jack' in this brilliant authorised biography which is presented in a foreword by Jack himself.

For the first time Jack's wife and family, his teammates as a World Cup winner with England in 1966, and his players during his management years with Middlesbrough, Sheffield Wednesday, Newcastle, and Ireland tell their stories of the man who dominated their lives.

Graeme Souness, Chris Waddle, and Peter Beardsley amongst others, are joined by Mick McCarthy, Niall Quinn and the greatest footballers who played under Big Jack for 10 years as Ireland team boss.

This is the most personable, inviting and intimate account of Jack Charlton's life, and the book contains photographs published for the first time from Jack and Pat Charlton's personal collection.

Jack Charlton: The Authorised Biography is written by former Daily Mail Northern Football Correspondent, Colin Young.

Author: Colin Young
Print Price: €20.00
Ebook: €10.00
ISBN: 9781910827017

Available on
Amazon

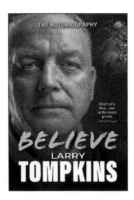

BELIEVE

Larry Tompkins: An Autobiography

HIS SELF-BELIEF WAS unbreakable.

His iron will inspirational.

Nothing could stop Larry Tompkins. No man, no team, as he made his football life the greatest story ever told in the long and brilliant history of the GAA.

Six years with his native Kildare left him empty-handed and heartbroken. He emigrated to New York to find a job and find a team he could lead to championship glory. In the United States, Tompkins' belief in himself never dimmed. He led Donegal to four New York championships in the Big Apple. He also found a new home for himself in Ireland and led Castlehaven to two Cork and Munster titles. In between, he also became the most valuable and feared footballer in Ireland.

BELIEVE is the story of a man who defied all the odds. In Cork's magnificent red shirt, he led his adopted county to two All-Ireland titles in 1989 and 90, one National League and six Munster titles, and he also was honoured with three Allstar awards.

Upon his retirement, Larry Tompkins continued to lead and inspire, and make others believe too. He managed Cork for seven years, winning Munster glory again, and drove Cork to the 1999 All-Ireland final where they agonisingly came up short.

BELIEVE is a story which proves to everyone, in every sport, that anything is possible and everything is there to be won!

Authors: Larry Tompkins with Denis Hurley
Print Price: €20.00
Ebook: €10.00
ISBN: 9781910827123

Available on

Amazon
Apple Books
Kobo

And all good online stores

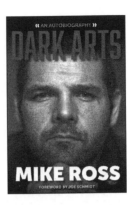

Dark Arts
Mike Ross: An Autobiography

FOR THE FIRST time, Mike Ross brings sports fans into the dark heart of the professional game of rugby union. Ross is recognised as the greatest scrummager in Irish rugby history – and the man who was the foundation stone for the beginning of the Joe Schmidt era, which saw Leinster win back-to-back Heineken Cups and Ireland become the greatest team in Europe.

But Mike Ross might never have been a professional rugby player. He did not turn pro until he was 26 years of age. And he spent three years learning his trade at the toughest end of the game with Harlequins in England before coming home at 30, and chasing the dream of an Irish jersey.

Ross would play 61 times for Ireland, and over 150 times for Leinster. His story is one of big dreams and amazing courage, on and off the field.

He writes about the good times and the hardest times, facing the true beasts of the professional game every weekend. And he writes about his own life, and the suicide of his younger brother, Andrew at 16 years of age with an honesty and compassion that is rewarding for everyone who has experienced the sudden death of a loved one and has to rebuild their lives.

Authors: Mike Ross with Liam Hayes
Print Price: €20.00
Ebook: €10.00
ISBN: 9781910827048

Available on
Amazon
Apple Books
Kobo
And all good online stores

GALWAY
GAME OF MY LIFE

TWENTY-FIVE OF Galway's greatest hurlers remember the one game that will live with them forever ...

including Jimmy Hegarty, Ned Dervan, Andy Fenton, Iggy Clarke, Sean Silke, Joe Connolly, PJ Molloy, Noel Lane, John Connolly, Mike Conneely, Anthony Cunningham, Pete Finnerty, Eanna Ryan, Gerry McInerney, John Commins, Michael Coleman, Micheál Donoghue, Padraig Kelly, Kevin Broderick, Ger Farragher, David Collins, Ollie Canning, Alan Kerins, Fergal Moore and Gearoid McInerney

... the day that defined their lives.

Author: Ollie Turner
Print Price: €20.00
Ebook: €9.99
ISBN: 9781910827284